The Day The Eagle Took Off

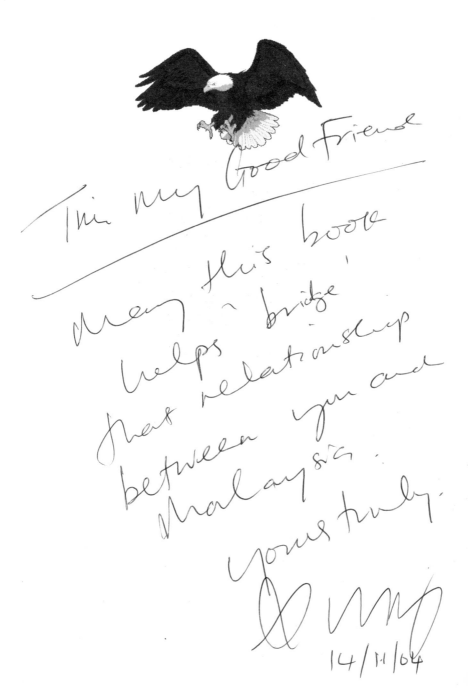

To my Good Friend

May this book
helps a bridge
that relationship
between you and
Malaysia.
yours truly.

14/11/04

Dreams Are Meant
For Those Who Have A
Purpose In Life...
And Those With A
Purpose In Life Shall
Find Infinite
Ways To Fulfil
Their Dreams

The Day The Eagle Took Off

David Goh

A Sterling Paperback

STERLING PAPERBACKS
An imprint of
Sterling Publishers (P) Ltd.
A-59 Okhla Industrial Area, Phase-II,
New Delhi-110020.
Tel: 26387070, 26386209; Fax: 91-11-26383788
E-mail: ghai@nde.vsnl.net.in
Website: www.sterlingpublishers.com

The Day The Eagle Took Off
© 2003, David Goh
Revised & Enlarged Edition 2003
ISBN: 81 207 2568 9
Formerly Titled: *Step Into The Future With Nothing*
First Edition 1993
Reprinted 1993-2000 (Nine times)

Published by Sterling Publishers Pvt. Ltd., New Delhi-110020.
Typeset by Vikas Compographics, New Delhi-110020.
Printed at Sai Early Learners Press (P) Ltd.

...in memory of my mother
(1901 – 1998)

Preface

"If you skip this page, you miss the objective of this book."
- The Author

Kenny was a good man, a loving husband and a great father to five kids.

He was a kindhearted, helpful individual, and wherever he went, everyone loved him dearly. He lived in a good neighbourhood, surrounded by good and gentle people. His employer adored him. He lived a life with no regrets, for he had never expected to prosper and had never asked for it either, so he was given exactly what he lived and worked for, no more…no less. Kenny never had too many good things in his life, but he was undoubtedly a happy man, even though he remained poor almost all through his life.

From the very beginning, even as a young boy, Kenny had wanted to fulfil his mother's dream, and that was to be a good Christian.

For Kenny, going to Heaven was the only important thing.

One night, shortly after his sixty-fourth birthday celebration, Kenny's time on earth came to an end. Although it was painful for his beloved family members, but Kenny had to go. And true to his mother's words, he found himself wandering in a peaceful place, acre after acre of peaceful surrounding. As he approached a gigantic gate, there was an angel waiting for him.

"You must be Kenny!" exclaimed the angel.

"Yes, and you are…?" Kenny was curious.

"I am your guardian angel. I will be accompanying you throughout your entire time here, after which you will be transported to another, lovelier place, but for now, let me show you around the courtyard of this peaceful sanctuary. I just want to ensure you become familiar with this courtyard. You can call me Richard."

"Where do I sleep?" asked the curious Kenny.

"Nobody sleeps in Heaven, you should know that by now Kenny," Richard was very courteous.

They must have walked for hours, but Kenny never felt tired at all, nor was he thirsty. Then they came to a huge mansion surrounded by an endless stone wall. The mansion was huge and magnificent; it stretched as far as his eyes could see. It must have had thousands of floors, each floor covered in gold to differentiate it from the other floors of the building. There was a grand staircase leading to the main entrance of the mansion. Each step on the staircase was engulfed in a thick layer of white clouds. Kenny could see the gold trimming on the knots surrounding the handrail, each knot a solid gold dove, standing proudly, its eyes beaming with the serene colour of love. Seven giant pillars of gold stood solidly in the passage to the grand staircase.

"What is this building, Richard?" asked Kenny.

"This is the mansion of eternity. You see this yellow line on the ground? Cross the yellow line, and you will be in Heaven. But you must not cross this yellow line until you are ordered to. For now, you shall spend some time here in the courtyard, Kenny, and while you are here, make the most of it," Richard warned.

"Give me your hand, Kenny." Richard commanded.

Kenny stretched out his hand and opened his palm. "Here, let me give you this..." said Richard, as he handed him a tablet, ruggedly rounded and looking like granite. Some numbers were etched on it.

The numbers were **1 19 11 – 6 15 18 – 9 20** Kenny scratched his head, wondering what they meant, but he didn't ask what the tablet was nor did he ask why it had been given to him.

"Keep the tablet close to you always, Kenny," Richard insisted.

Kenny, quickly put it in his pocket.

"Thank you, Richard," as usual, Kenny was courteous.

Time passes quickly in the courtyard. Kenny's friendship with Richard grew. Before long, Kenny was able to find his way around the courtyard and on many occasions, he came to the edge of the courtyard, stood behind the yellow line, admiring the big mansion. However, Kenny dared not pass the yellow line which divided the courtyard and Heaven. He remembered the stern warning from Richard not too long ago.

"If you cross this yellow line before your time, you must face the consequence of returning to where you began from. You have laboured hard to gain entry to the courtyard, so don't go spoiling your entire lifetime's work."

One morning, Kenny and Richard were walking beside a lake and, from a distance, Kenny saw a huge wooden hut. "Why is a wooden hut here?" he asked.

"Never mind about the wooden hut, Kenny, we have plenty to accomplish today," Richard tried to distract Kenny's attention from the wooden hut. Kenny tried hard to take his mind off the old wooden hut, but it kept haunting him, day after day.

"Richard, I want to learn more about the wooden hut. Could we go there today?" asked Kenny.

"The wooden hut is nothing but a memory of the past, you don't want to go there, Kenny," Richard was patient.

"What is stored in the memory of the past?" Kenny became more curious.

"The wooden hut keeps a record of all human beings, what they had asked for and what was given," Richard said. "It is of no importance now, Kenny."

"Do you have all the answers to the questions I will be asked when I meet the Almighty?" Kenny asked Richard.

"What would you like to know, Kenny?" Richard asked. "Well, for one thing, I am sure the Almighty would like to know what you accomplished when he first sent you to earth." Richard continued.

Kenny tilted his head upwards as if searching for an answer.

"Frankly, Richard, I didn't accomplish much. Though I successfully brought up my family the way my mother had wanted me to, we were really not happy because we lacked certain things," Kenny confirmed.

"And may I ask what was always missing?" Richard asked.

"To begin with…I think, I am always lagging behind. Most of my friends got to achieve many wonderful things in life. They lived in bigger houses than mine, drove bigger cars, had plenty of opportunities which I was denied most of the time. I used to wonder whether they were better than I, smarter than I or simply luckier than I," Kenny answered.

"Kenny, to be fair to you, I think everyone should at least begin life with a deeper understanding of oneself. In the game of life, success or failure is really up to the individual. The world is, of course, a stage, the men and women are the actors, and everyone is playing some part in the production of life's harmony. Some, as you already know, are just spectators. They sit and watch the great stage of life at work, staring with admiration at the men and women who are performing. But then again, there are also some who watch these performers with intense jealousy, for they feel that since they can't be on the stage, others shouldn't be there either. Evidently, I think the saddest of all are those who are neither here nor there," Richard began his philosophical lesson.

"What do you mean by neither here nor there?" Kenny asked.

"These are the mass of individuals living in the world like hamsters. They just go round and round like a spinning wheel, never seem to get anywhere, and at last, exhausted, find themselves exactly where they began.

"These are the people who lived in a world they thought was complete...at least, it was to them. They look nice on the outside, but on the inside, they are insufficient in all areas. They may look successful, but in reality, they are far from it, they may look radiant, however, on the inside, they are just incompetent. You see, Kenny, the Almighty didn't put you somewhere where you would be the victim of circumstances, to be tossed about by some cruel fate, regardless of your own effort..." Richard was in control.

Kenny asked surprisingly, "What does He expect from us?"

"The Almighty has given you existence, with full power and the opportunity to improve it and be happy. Everyone was born with an equal distribution of power – the power of choice. Kenny, you were given this power to choose between success and failure, to be happy or sad, to be a leader or a follower, to be good or bad, gentle or crude, and along with many other wonderful choices, He gave us this power to choose the route to the goodness of mankind or the uneven path of evil," Richard explained further.

"With this power of choice, if people know the importance of choice, then why are there so many failures Richard?" Kenny queried.

"Simple. Like I told you earlier, even though men and women were given the power to choose, most people tend to take the shortest cut in life, they want to be very rich, but don't put in their full effort, thus, they take the short cut to financial freedom. Some cheat and rob, and a few kill others in order to grab the bag of money they think can provide them financial freedom.

"To achieve financial freedom is bliss. The Almighty wants everyone to enjoy this success, certainly, but He doesn't want people to take any other route except the one that He has planned for – and that is to work for it!

"People wish for a happy family, but don't take the time to build one or to understand the feelings of loved ones. How can one achieve happiness within the family without spending time at home? How can two persons shape a family toward the happiness they desire, if one party keeps on taking and the other party keeps on giving? Soon, the giver will get tired and, eventually, give up.

"Everyone yearns for a cleaner and better world to live in. This has become a global issue. Remember, the Almighty gave this world life, and now people are destroying that life by poisoning it with pollution, the ozone layer is getting destroyed, oxygen is getting mixed with poisonous gas. Trees, that cool the earth, are now being cut to pieces to make way for development, rivers are being turned into dumping grounds. The whole world is now a polluted celestial body. People simply take the shortest cut to fulfil their dreams without any regard for others. Kenny, we can't have the world going on in this manner, it would simply slow down the process and one day – Armageddon. The world would come to an end. And you know something, Kenny? It doesn't have to end this way. If only people would learn to live a more peaceful, and harmonious life, be patient, determined, caring, sharing, giving and thoughtful. These are the things that create the spirit of human happiness," Richard explained meticulously to Kenny.

"Richard, what do you know about achieving unlimited successes?" Kenny asked further, "Some of my friends and also others have achieved the ultimate success, and in so doing, they have left behind them a successful legacy. What makes these people so successful?"

"If only you had asked these questions before you came to the courtyard, you would have achieved the ultimate successes yourself," Richard answered. "However, let me explain... You see, every man, woman and child has infinite potential, just waiting to be tapped. The Almighty has planted this potential within you, and all you have to do is believe in yourself. That you are special and created for a special purpose, and believe you are worthy of every single breath you inhale, and every single step you take." Richard went on, "Too many people live pretentiously in the world. They want to feel they are okay, but in reality they are not. They want to look good outside, but do not bother about the inside. What makes it worse is the fact that they know about their inadequacy but do nothing to overcome it," Richard concluded.

"Does this mean false pride?" Kenny pressed further.

"You got it, Kenny!" Richard answered.

It was days later that Kenny again found himself near the lake, looking at the wooden hut. He could not contain his curiosity and approached the wooden hut with confidence. When he came to the main entrance of the wooden hut, he found a door, which had no frame, nor a handle to push it open or shut. Kenny checked further. Strangely enough the door had no hinges either. "How can a door stand on its own without a door-frame and hinges," he wondered. "I guess that's how things are in Heaven," he thought.

He tried to open the door by pushing it, but it didn't move an inch. Then he tried to grip the door by pulling it instead, but the door just wouldn't open. Finally, he gave up and turned away.

"I was at the wooden hut the other day," Kenny told Richard.

"You were? And what did you discover?" Richard asked.

"Nothing! It's just a strange old door, standing on its own. I tried to push it and then I tried to pull it open, nothing works," Kenny expressed his frustration.

"Just how do you open the door Richard?" Kenny wanted to know.

"I am your guardian angel, I am not suppose to give you everything you ask for; however, sensing your frustration, I well assist you to some extent," Richard assured him.

"Well, how do I get it opened then?" Kenny pressed on.

"First, you should ask, then seek and knock. And that's all I can tell you, I can't show how it is done. Now, if you really want to know what is inside the wooden hut, get moving. But I can't go in there with you," Richard continued.

Ask, Seek and Knock. Kenny tried to memorise the three words. "What shall I ask?" he wondered.

Once again, he came to the wooden hut, "Ask. Ask what?" Then he thought, "what do I want at this moment of time, right this very minute. To get the door open—that's it, ask for the door to be opened." He had found his answer.

"Please open this door." He felt a little silly asking no one in particular.

Suddenly, a voice came from nowhere. " Why do you want this door opened?"

"I want to get in there. And who are you?" Kenny was curious.

"I am the post angel guarding the house of memory of the past," said the voice.

"Open the door, please." Kenny sounded humble.

Suddenly, there was a click, and the door opened. Kenny could only watch in amazement. When he finally pushed open the door, he could see stack upon stack of wooden boxes with names written on them. There were designs beautifully crafted on each side of the mahogany wooden boxes. They were properly stacked high up, in hundreds of levels. "What's inside these boxes?" He asked.

"Why do you want to know?" the angel questioned.

"Because I want to know if my box is here in this wooden hut?" Kenny craved for an answer.

"Sure! Your box is somewhere around. Do you wish to look for it?" the voice came back.

"Yes, I demand to see my box now." Kenny knew exactly what to say and how to say it.

Almost immediately, a box appeared in front of him, with his name engraved on the top. He tried to open it, and again he felt the same frustration that he had felt when he had tried opening the door earlier.

"I ask to open the box now," he commanded. But nothing happened.

Where did I go wrong? He asked himself. Then he recalled how Richard had instructed him: To Ask, to Seek and To Knock.

Since this is the last stage, I should just go ahead and knock on the wooden box, he thought to himself.

Kenny knocked three times on top of the wooden box with his knuckles. Suddenly, the lid of the box began to open slightly. Kenny tried to prise open the lid.

When the lid was finally opened, Kenny took a closer look into the box. And then, Kenny's face went pale. His hands trembling, Kenny began to cry, "This can't be true...No, this can't be true!"

Kenny ran out of the wooden hut and went to see Richard. "Oh no, this can't be true, Richard. How could this be? How can the memory of the past come back to shock me in this way? Explain, please," begged Kenny.

"Kenny, the things you saw in the wooden box are the greatest gifts the Almighty had promised to give each of his children, and all you had to do was to ask Him for it. You see, you never asked Him for anything. You were a good Christian, but in order to live a life filled with riches, you need to demand from Him. The things you saw in the chest, such as big houses, beautiful cars, gold bars and all those precious ornaments and cash, and the happiness that you deserved, things that can provide your children happiness, peace of mind, all of them...are your inheritance, all you need to do is ask for them. But you didn't. Your greatest mistake in life was to live a life with no demands, so you received what life offered you, and you accepted it even though you are eligible for the finer things in life. Yes, Kenny, in other words, you have short - changed yourself. You lived a life of mediocrity. Life is not a bargain. It is a bill of demand. Demand what is rightfully yours, and it shall be given eventually," Richard said.

Richard instructed Kenny to take out the tablet that he had given him earlier. Kenny reached into his pocket and, uncomfortably, he took it out and handed it over to Richard. "See these figures; **1 19 11 – 6 15 18 – 9 20,**

Well, Kenny if you were to turn the numbers into ABC, you will get the answer. A=1 B=2, of course Z=26."

I have repeated this story many times in the past, over the years as a motivational speaker. *The Day The Eagle Took Off* is about demanding what is rightfully yours. First, you have to believe in yourself. Next, you have to believe in Almighty God, and, finally, you have to believe that the things you ask for shall be given to you wholeheartedly.

Believe me, when I was hitting my head against the wall on numerous occasions, I would bleed, cry and curse, but nothing good came of it. It wasn't until I began to make demands from God for the things I deserved that things got better and better. Know your own human rights, what is rightfully yours, and ask God for it. As promised in Psalms 2:8 "Ask of me, and I will make the nations your heritage, and the ends of the earth your possession." Yes, He will gladly give them to you. And, finally, believe that He will give them to you.

God bless you always,

22 Jalan, 1/1 Villa Heights   ***David Goh***
43000 Kajang, Selangor Darul Ehsan   ***Isaiah 40 : 31***
Malaysia
Tel.: (603) 8734 7300, Fax: (603) 8734 7090
E-mail: davidg@tm.net.my

Contents

A284315

KEMENTERIAN PELAJARAN MALAYSIA

SIJIL RENDAH PELAJARAN

Bahawa sa-nya ini-lah di-nyatakan chalun yang tersebut nama-nya di-bawah telah mengambil pepereksaan untok sijil yang tersebut di-atas dalam bulan Oktober 1969, dan telah menchapai sa-kurang 2-nya perengkat 8 dalam mata-pelajaran atau mata2-pelajaran yang tertulis di-bawah dengan perengkat yang di-perolehi-nya di-tunjokkan di-hujong tiap2 mata-pelajaran itu.

GOH CHAI WHATT

SEKOLAH MENENGAH INGGERIS
PORT DICKSON NEGERI SEMBILAN

ENGLISH I	7	(LULUS)
ENGLISH II	7	(LULUS)
HISTORY	7	(LULUS)
MATHEMATICS I	8	(LULUS)
SCIENCE I	7	(LULUS)
ART	8	(LULUS)
	44 points	

SIJIL PANGKAT — C
JUMLAH MATA2 PELAJARAN — ENAM
MENERUSI PERANTARAAN BAHASA INGGERIS

ANGKA GILIRAN 10181045

Pengawal Pepereksaan,
Kementerian Pelajaran, Malaysia.

Chap Lembaga Pepereksaan.

1

My World Came to a Standstill

"Oh, my God... I failed my L.C.E. (Lower Certificate of Education) examination!

It came as a shock, like a bolt of lightning streaking across the dark sky. Relentlessly, I paced up and down the school corridors in Sekolah Menegah Inggeris, Port Dickson. That was in 1970, I had gone to the school to get my much-awaited results.

My world came to a standstill. I was barely 17 years old. I guess it was really too much of a shock to realise that I would be confined to a world of rejection. At that moment of my life, I felt that I was a 'rejected specimen' of society... a failure.

What would my friends think of me? Worse still, what would my mother say or do? These and other questions about my present and future raced across my mind and filled me with trepidation.

I must have sat in the middle of the school field for hours, not knowing where and how to start, fearful as I was. For hours, I wept silently. I stayed away from my school and classmates for fear they would see my insecurity, and my crushed ego. It must have been the sun's heat that finally forced me to pluck up my courage, to stand up and walk away from the school compound. For the last time, I turned to look at the school, bidding good-bye to the place that had once brought me so much joy, knowing well that I would never return.

At that age, what could I possibly do? I was still dependent on others, what could I really do for myself? Desperate, fearful and unsure, I plied the streets of Port Dickson daily. Well, at least one thing was for sure, this was the beginning, though a bleak one, and having realised that, there was only one thing left to be done – work. I had to get out, to work, to earn a living. It would not be easy. I would have to forgo a lot of things: the fun of visiting friends, going around laughing with schoolmates, the joy of travelling in a school bus, and most of all, the enjoyable carefree life of a student.

WHAT YOU THINK ABOUT ALL DAY DETERMINES WHAT YOU ARE

There must be hundreds of books written on the subject of YOU ARE WHAT YOU THINK YOU ARE. One of the earliest such books was written by a mysterious man named James Allen. His inspirational classic, *AS A MAN THINKETH*, has literally inspired millions of people.

POWER OF THOUGHT BRINGS FAME, FORTUNE AND HAPPINESS

James Allen believed in the power of thought to bring fame, fortune and happiness. He wrote:

> *As a being of power, intelligence, and love, and the lord of his own thoughts, man holds the key to every situation, and has within himself the means of transforming himself into what he wills. Whatever a man achieves or fails to achieve is the direct result of his own thoughts.*

Our mental attitude toward the objective we are struggling for, has everything to do with our attaining it. If you want to become prosperous, you must first believe that you are made for success and happiness: that there is a divinity in you that will, if you follow it, bring you into the light of prosperity. Erase all shadows of doubts and fears, and any suggestion of poverty and failure from the ocean of your mind. When you have become the master of your own thoughts, when you have learned to dominate your mind, you will be on the road to success. Discouragement, fear, doubt and lack of self-confidence are the germs that have killed the prosperity and happiness of millions of people.

Not too long ago, when I shared the platform with Dr Denis Waitely, America's most distinguished motivational teacher, he said, "Poverty is untested potential, resulting from self-imposed limitation."

What Dr Denis Waitely was trying to say is exactly what others have been trying to say all these decades – You Are What You Think You Are. The world makes way for the determined individual, and obstacles stay out of the path of the determined, unchangeable soul. People who achieve great things in life are powerful in their affirmations. They have an absolute positive attitude, never changing. They never give up nor give in to the negative circumstances they come across.

You Become What You Think About

Dr William James once stated, "Man can change his attitude by changing what he thinks about." Yes, evidently, we are the sum total of all our thoughts. Therefore, it is important that we carefully consider what we think about. Select good, clean, powerful and rich thoughts before you put them into your head.

You must have heard of the term GIGO which stands for Garbage In, Garbage Out. If someone keys in the wrong information or wrong data, then, automatically, the wrong information or wrong data will be shown on the monitor when you try to retrieve it.

Our brain functions exactly like a computer. When good thoughts are stored, good things will emerge when you need them. Similarly, if you put in evil thoughts, then unrighteousness will soon dominate and control you. We reflect in our behaviour what we keep in our mind, so we should use this mental picture as an opportunity to acquire a new self and re-evaluate our values.

When you wake up in the morning, go to the bathroom and look into the mirror. If you don't like what you see in the mirror, don't worry. Remember, you are not stuck with you, for you can change...only through your own thoughts.

Change begins with thoughts, and then actions follow. I call this an attitude of mind. As a motivational speaker since 1977, I have met countless individuals, both negative and positive, and I must say, there is a great difference between these two groups of people. Let us divide these two into A &

B Groups. People of A Group are positive while those of B Group are negative.

Let us examine and make a comparison between the characteristics of their attitudes:

Positive	Negative
Can be done	Can't be done
Overcoming weakness	It's a lousy idea, it won't work
Open to new suggestions	Sceptical about suggestions
Looking at the bright side	Looking at the dark side
Generous	Petty
Praise	Condemn and complain
Hope builder	Hope destroyer
Giver	Taker
Uplifting others	Belittling others
Problem solver	Problem creator
Talking about change	Talking about others (gossip)

Positive people, by and large, end up as winners in life, while negative people, in most cases, lose out. Usually, they end up scooping up what is left over by the positive group of people. I have had the opportunity to witness many cases of both negative and positive development of people. And I have also seen how positive people turn around negative situations to their advantage.

Cancer patients are advised by their doctors to think positively in order to expedite the healing process.

Hundreds of thousands of dollars are spent on medical bills weekly, monthly or yearly by some patients. The amounts vary with the degree of self-worth, and net-worth of each individual. Kerry Packer, the billionaire in Australia, could spend a million dollars on his medical bill, and it wouldn't make a dent in his wallet while an average fellow may get a heart-attack, when he finds out that his surgeon has just slapped him a five-thousand dollar bill. Drugs and surgeons' professional fees are ridiculously exorbitant these days. Well, thanks to science and technology. But there is a wonderful, drug-free approach that heals better, faster and there is, literally, no professional fee involved. It is called **the healthy attitude of mind.**

No, please don't get me wrong. I am not suggesting that you can do away with doctors or surgeons. I am only suggesting that along with their assistance, we also need to think positively. Frankly, a patient will not be properly cured if she spends half the time in her sick bed thinking that she is going to die or that something awful is about to happen. You know what? She is right, something awful will happen!

Religious teachers may not agree with what I am about to say, but the objective and intention is to illustrate the drawing power of our mind and not to argue about where the power comes from.

Between the power of the mind, and the operating force of the universe, I believe there is a connection. That's what the term *like attracts like means*. Basically, like it or not, we are constantly attracting both the seen and unseen forces of life. Likewise there are positive and negative forces. These forces are akin to the power of our mind.

For instance, if you grow up in a group of negative people, the chances are that you will have a negative approach to solving your challenges. These are the seen forces.

Let's touch on the unseen forces: in the past, we have heard stories and newspaper reports about certain spiritual leaders in and outside our country who used the negative approach in their worship or teachings. Many of them sacrificed animals as part of their worship. A few of them went to the extreme of sacrificing human being. People questioned whether there was any truth in their worship and teachings. The answer is found in their beliefs. If you believe that the unseen force is working for you and not against you, the chances are great that you will continue to believe in it. All I am trying to illustrate is the belief in a force, be it negative or positive, and this is not a matter of morals so don't get confused here.

As long as you believe that the force is working for you, the more you believe, the stronger your conviction is going to be. The deeper the conviction is felt, the more you will be obsessed. Soon, the negative approach will eventually become the truth – your truth!

That's how you get to read in the papers that young girls and boys are tortured and killed for religious beliefs. Of course the authorities are not going to compromise on any such approach because they believe that no one should play God; one can worship God, but not play God. In the first place, no one should take away someone else's life, when God was the one who gave life.

Similarly, there are positive forces in this universe that you can tap, which can be of great help to you, any time in your life. I can't tell you where these positive forces come from, but I do know they are there for you to tap. When you cognate the positive forces with the drawing power of your mind, you form one of the most powerful positive alliances in the world. Nothing can come in your way.

Your journey to success is guaranteed.

So, it is a matter of your thinking... your belief.
If you think you are well, you are.
If you think you can win, you can.
If you think of peace, peace shall come upon you.
If you think of love, then you shall be loved.
If you think you can, you can.
If you think you are successful, you almost certainly will be.
If you think you are pretty, you are.
If you think you are unique, then you shall be.
If you think positive, you will act positively.
If you think you can close the sale, you can.

On the other hand, if you chose to think otherwise, then also, you are right. Like I said earlier, you are the sum total of what you think about.
If you think evil, you will act evil.
If you think you are unworthy, you are.
If you think you are a failure, then you are.
If you think you are negative, you will end up losing more.
If you think you are hopeless, then you are.
If you think you won't make it, the chances are you won't!

Thinking, and believing, is an essential part of mental training. For example, the antidote for any amount of human ills can be the magical chemistry of positive thinking. It is a cure for greed, jealousy, hatred, envy, revenge, criminal intention and other self-destructive emotions. Think what would be the result, if we could keep our minds filled with loving, helpful, hopeful, encouraging, cheerful and other fearless suggestions.

We would not then need to deny the opposition, for when the positive is present, the negative disappears!

Remember, every true, helpful thought is in fact a cell; if held in the mind, it will reproduce there. It will clarify the ideals and uplift your life. While you fill your mind with these inspiring, helpful, and beautiful thoughts, the opposition will disappear, because you leave no room for negativism. How do you drive darkness out of a room? You let the light in, don't you? How do you drive the hatred that filled your mind? You let in love, and hatred will naturally be driven out sooner or later. Change your mental attitude – think win, think love, think peace, think harmony, and the opposition will be instantly withdrawn.

Since negative thinking – such as jealousy, hatred, conflict, egoism, loss, killing, dying, trouble, etc – is bad, why are there so many negative people around, and where do they adopt this kind of destructive attitude? The world is filled with many negative people, but unfortunately, not all of them realise that being negative is bad, because it has never been highlighted, and they do not know how detrimental it is.

Adopting a negative attitude can begin at a very young age. People get trained from a young, tender age. They may have learnt the lesson from their parents, teachers, and classmates, and as they grew older, they began to get the negative lessons from newspapers. If you look at the newspapers today, you will find that at least 80% of the news covered is negative, and people actually like to read such negative news.

"Hold it David, are you saying, reading the newspaper contaminates the mind?" you may ask. "Of course, the newspaper not only provides you news of what happened yesterday, it also influences you a great deal. Do you know that when you read some false information daily, it will eventually become the truth? It is a subliminal approach towards the objective. That's why the newspaper business is still one of the best businesses to get into." That would be my answer.

Not too long ago, I came to know about a newspaper in the US several decades ago that reported only good news, and you know what? It couldn't survive for long. It went out of business within a short period of time. People generally like to read the bad news; the more dramatic the bad news is, the more paper the will sell. That explains why people are generally negative in their attitude.

Never look at the dark side; take a sunny view of everything. The people I have seen succeed in life have always been cheerful and hopeful, they went about their business with a smile on their faces, and took chances at every step. They are optimistic in every sense of the word.

THE POSITIVE PEOPLE THAT I KNOW...

I Went Out There With A Positive Attitude

18 April, 1999 may seem like an ordinary day to you and to many people around the world. But it marked a historic achievement for a Malaysian, Captain Datuk Azhar Mansor. For on that day, he completed an ultimate challenge – Langkawi to Langkawi Solo Round the World Record in 190 days, 6 hours, 57 minutes and 2 seconds. This achievement was recognised by the World Sailing Speed Record Council as a world record. He had sailed non-stop around the world single-handedly. "When you attempt to sail around the world, the World Sailing Speed Record Council will require you to take the route where no ocean liner goes," said Captain Datuk Azhar.

However, he ran into a storm which damaged his boat somewhere near Falklands, forcing him to make a stopover. "I went out there with a positive mental attitude. There was no doubt in my mind that I would not come back to Langkawi, because that's where my heart is. Although some parts of the boat were damaged, but not my spirit," he said on 13 March 2001 at the Genting Highlands Resort. Later in the day, when we had lunch at the restaurant, I asked Captain Datuk Azhar, "What advice can you give to young aspiring Malaysians?"

"Be positive, and act positively!" he said.

Proved! With positive thinking, you can accomplish anything you wish to.

Looking at the AIA Building

I have been on the speaking platform with Jeffrey Chiew on several occasions. He never fails to inspire me every time. An old-timer in the life insurance industry, his name is inscribed in the hearts of every life insurance agent around the world.

"I'd like to do a story on you Jeff," I told him one day.

He agreed, and the appointment was set at the Regent of Kuala Lumpur. He arrived ahead of schedule. "I always try to be a little early for every appointment, David," he was courteous.

Born in a family of eight, and being the youngest, he had on several occasions worked with his father. "My father was a petty trader, he would collect used cardboards, clean them and resell them to whoever needed them. That's what my father did for a living. Yes, I was raised in a poor family."

Jeffrey lived with his parents in a slum, their house was an old wooden shack, facing the tallest building - the AIA building.

"AIA was once the tallest building in Kuala Lumpur," he quipped. The room he stayed in had a window that had a clear view of the AIA building, and every morning, Jeffrey would sit by the bed and look out the window, at the executives wearing ties, long sleeved shirts, some in suits. Many of them came in big, fancy cars. Some were chauffeured to work. He looked at them with admiration and fascination.

"I hope one day to work in that tall building," Jeffrey thought to himself.

Young Jeff would sit by his mother's side daily, accompanying her while she did her daily chores. Occasionally, he would peep out of the window and look at the executives and that fascinating building, and he would start daydreaming again.

To cut the story short, Jeffrey went into the life insurance business at the age of 19 as a part-time agent, and the rest was history. Now after more than two decades of life insurance, and with a string of honours, from being the top agent in the company to AIA Ambassador, he sits on the board of many life insurance councils and associations. One can easily figure out that he is today one of those multi-millionaires who have made it good in the industry.

"I had been trampled, chased out from people's offices, and had been branded as the worst salesman in the world...but I just kept going, not giving in, with a positive mental attitude," he said.

"Every once in a while, I still look out of the window from my AIA office, searching for a wooden shack somewhere nearby...wondering if there is a young boy, somewhere, looking at the AIA office..." Jeffrey mused.

Today, Jeffrey is considered one of the very best in the industry. His charismatic presentation skill keeps his audience spell-bound every time.

Proved! With positive thinking you can become rich. It has nothing to do with your past. It is today, now and tomorrow. Think positively.

No Time to Think About Failure

He took time and built it into a household name – Honda. The man who was responsible for bringing Honda cars into our country, Tan Sri Loh Boon Siew, a self-made billionaire, a philanthropist, and a friend to many. According to his version, the story of Honda in Malaysia began when he took a vacation to Japan when he was 43 years old. While in Osaka, Japan, he saw a man riding an amazing machine that he had never seen before. He chased after that man, and finally after catching up with him, he learned that the machine was a motorcycle. Today, every living being in this country knows what a Honda is.

Loh Boon Siew left China at the tender age of 12, for what was then British Malaya. His first job was as an apprentice mechanic in a workshop. Survival was the name of the game. He worked day and night, washing cow dung, and dirt off the bodies and tyres of buses. Sheer hard work, but he was determined to make it. He saved every cent he earned, and obviously, he had no time to think about failure. By 1933, when he was 18, young Loh had managed to save $12,000. He was good at his job so people came to him from afar. He would service cars and buses until past midnight daily. Thinking positively, Loh became enterprising and set up his own automobile repair shop. He sold bicycle parts. Later, he became a used-car dealer. By the time he was 41, he was already widely acclaimed in Penang as a "towkay" (boss). He owned 40 buses that he no longer needed to wash and clean himself.

Eventually, Loh met the founder of Honda, Mr Soichiro Honda. They remained good friends for well over 30 years until Honda died several years ago. Before the turn of the 21st century, Tan Sri Loh Boon Siew passed away, his death left a void in many Malaysian lives. Literally, thousands turned up to pay their last respects.

Proved! Positive thinking widens the horizon of wealth and unlimited opportunities.

I really do not need to go into the many cases just to prove that positive thinking works. The last three cases have given me enough evidence and I hope you are convinced as well.

Sharing the components of success through the development of a positive attitude is my objective in this chapter. I strongly suggest that you do something about it. After all, if you are striving for success, why don't you try to adopt some of these attitudes? These words will be of invaluable help to you as they have been designed specially for people who want more out of life:

Achievement	Proud	Persistence
Success	Motivated	Best
Determination	Effectiveness	Extra Effort
Desire	Success	Result
I Can	I Will	Opportunity
Challenging	Love	Care
Smile	High Performance	Enthusiasm
Recognition	Zest	Confidence
Go-Getter	Go For It	Principles
Character	Happiness	Faith
	Forgiveness	

If the world can be filled with more people who apply and practise some of the above words, it will be a better place to live in.

The first time I met Zig Ziglar was in 1982. I was a young speaker then, and the first time I attended his *Born To Win* seminar was an amazing experience. In the seminar, I learned the song Born To Win as well. The words left a deep impression on me, and for as long as I live, the words shall remain within me.

"WE CAN MAKE THIS WORLD
A BETTER PLACE
IT BEGINS WITH YOU AND ME..."

Here's How You Can Develop to Become More Positive

Ever wonder why some people are so positive despite their negative surroundings? No one is born with a positive mental attitude, but somewhere deep within, the individual has to learn the lesson—it could be from parents, from self-help books, from peers, bosses or, simply, the positive friends he moves around with.

I have listed a few steps here to enable you to have a quick start-up in tuning your attitude to become more positive. These steps are the results of my 25 years' experience as a motivational speaker, and I am sure they will be as helpful to you as they are to me.

Invest in Brain Power

One of the most economical ways of tuning your attitude is investing in your brain power. Brain power techniques come from the psychosomatic approach. The term 'psychosomatic' means mental disorder. Do you know that there are many patients in hospitals today who are suffering because their minds tell them to suffer? Physically there is nothing wrong with some of these patients, but because of their worrisome attitude, they keep saying that something is wrong with a certain part of their body, and when they begin to tap the negative forces from the universe which is akin to the drawn power of the mind, it will create an explosion, as I have mentioned earlier in the chapter. We can also use the same approach: psychosomatically, can tap the positive forces from the universe and benefit ourselves. To begin with, you need to memorise these easy steps. Do this daily; repeat the following statements, by whispering to yourself. Or you can say them a little lower, but without disturbing others. You can do this in your car while you are on your way to see a client, or in the shower, or by the boat. Don't brag about this approach to others, for they will not understand, and will intimidate you unintentionally. Here are some statements you can begin with:

Yes, I can!
Yes, I will!
Yes, I must!
I feel happy and I am happy!
I feel good, and I feel great!
I am positive in every way!
This day is the best day of my life!
I am successful, and I can achieve more!

Do it for the next 100 days and feel the difference.

Warning: Don't do it because you think it is your duty to do so, do it because you feel like doing it.

Eschew

If you are really serious about getting better control of your life, begin now to be more selective about your friends. In the past, you were not consciously selecting your friends; now you need to do so. For some of these friends of yours have unknowingly pulled you down. And to some extent, they are the stumbling block to your gateway to success. These are what I have earlier termed the negative forces that flow around you. They say things that may have a major negative influence these are some of the things or statements that you aren't aware of but which are hurting you from within:

You can't do it!
You will fail!
You won't make it!
Don't make a fool of yourself!
You are a born loser!

'Eschew' means to abstain from. Learn to eschew these negative friends of yours. Be more conscious of the people you mix with daily. What they say sometimes may not hurt you physically, and you may just laugh over it, but mentally, the damage can be quite ambiguous.

Bite Your Tongue

Most people are generally jealous of their friends' success. As a result of that, the average person tends to say negative things or remarks about others. Psychologically, it may put you in a comfort-zone when you put others down, but it is one of the most self-damaging, subliminal messages that you can inflict upon yourself. Learn to bite your tongue. Stop yourself from making negative remarks about others. You don't have to be an 'expert' in order to look good. Let me give you examples of some of these damaging remarks:

The food here tastes horrible or
The deco here is horrible...

You have probably overheard statements like this, or perhaps you have even said such things yourself. However, some people like to say such things all the time, wherever they go, it makes them feel 'authorised,' makes them feel like as though they are experts in the field. Of course, there are some places where the food is horrible or the decor of the premises is bad, but do we really want to express that negativism in us, do we really want to go on damaging ourselves? We can put it another way, in a more refined manner; "the food here...well, one man's meat is another man's poison." Instead of the negative approach, bite your tongue and add some laughter. Or you can choose to bite your tongue and not make any remark. If others are saying it, you can always portray that positive attitude of yours by adding, "these are quite different, aren't they?"

When you do that, the impression you leave behind is tremendous, and the good impact you have on yourself is ten-fold.

You should have placed your windows here instead of there

Think for a while. A window is cast in the concrete or brick wall, and the proud owner would have paid hundreds or thousands of dollars for it, and here someone comes along, thinking like an 'architect', making comments. If the owner wanted a comment, he would have got it from a professional. He certainly doesn't need it from an amateur. I had the opportunity to witness this scenario several years ago; I was invited to a friend's house-warming party, he had just got his bungalow built on a nice piece of land. The huge bungalow had eight large bedrooms, three living rooms and a large dining hall. My friend had spent more than a hundred thousand dollars on the most hi-tech, state-of-the-art, modern kitchen. There were eight bathrooms, each of them tastefully decorated. There were approximately 80 people invited to this party, and all were enjoying themselves. I couldn't help but overhear this conversation between my friend, the owner of this bungalow and one of his guests; "Jimmy, you should place your window over there instead of here..." indicating where he thought a window was wrongly placed.

My friend tried to explain why the window was placed there, but, the conversation went on and on, until the architect who had designed the bungalow came and chipped in. "My friend, the owner of this mansion has spent 4.5 million dollars on it, and you are trying to say something is not quite right. I can't believe you said this." The architect shut everybody up. It was quite a show there.

Learn to bite your tongue. Say the positive things and leave the negative ones out. If you don't like the place that you are visiting, then vanish! Stop offending others, and be welcomed everywhere, any time.

Read Self-Help Books

Reading self-help books will provide you education. It is an exercise to widen your knowledge. Read books that can teach you good values. My life was turned around with the help of these books. And till today, I testify to the value of reading good books. My life was propelled upwards the moment I started reading lots of self-help books. Did I read a lot? Not really, just about 10-15 books a year. Here is a list of books I think you can begin with:

The Greatest Miracle In The World – *Og Mandino*
Life is Tremendous – *Charlie Jones*
See You At The Top – *Zig Ziglar*
The Secret of Success – *James Allen*
As A Man Thinketh – *James Allen*
I Dare You – *William Danfoth*
Jonathan Livingstone Seagull – *Richard Bach*
The Gifted Child – *Dr Paul Witty*
The Power of Positive Thinking – *Dr Norman Vincent Peale*
Think and Grow Rich – *Dr Napoleon Hill*
How To Win Friends and Influence People – *Dale Carnegie*

Acres of Diamond – *Russel Conwell*
The Law of Success – *Dr Napoleon Hill*
Secrets of a Top Sales Performer – *David Goh*
Blueprint For Greater Success – *David Goh*
From Zero to Millions –LKH Story – *David Goh*

How do you develop the reading habit? A number of people have asked me this question. Frankly, it is important that you start off by reading the right book. Why do you think some people just don't have the habit of reading? It is because they think all books are the same – hard to absorb, boring and with a the vocabulary that is difficult to understand.

That's why it is important that you read the right book in the beginning. I have personally read all the books mentioned above, all of them have been carefully written with the full intention of giving readers the motivation to flip though the pages. I hope you enjoy reading those self-help books as much as I do.

WITHOUT PAIN,

YOU CAN'T EXPERIENCE JOY

WITHOUT TASTING

THE BITTERNESS OF HARDSHIP

YOU CAN'T ENJOY

THE SWEETNESS OF LIFE

2

Life is Tough...

Before I wrote this book, then called *Step Into The Future With Nothing* a decade ago, I had a talk with my editor, Mark Wright. He was convinced that I had an inspiring story to share, and when the book was published, I showed it to my mother, who too was convinced that I had a good story to share. And of course, Times Publisher, my first publisher, had shared the same opinion. Subsequently, when the copyright was bought back from Times, I went into my own reprint and, to date, more than 350,000 copies are in the hands of many Malaysians, Singaporeans, Australians, New Zealanders, Indonesians, Thais, Canadians, Americans, Indians and so many others that I find it almost impossible to name them all. I have in our home, file after file of testimonies from people of all ages, races, and colours expressing their satisfaction and joy about this book, and how the book has uplifted their spirit and helped them to go out and strive for more in life.

My story is just another average Malaysian-turned-good story. And it is without any intention of being boastful that I have published this story. I have three objectives in this story.

To Inspire, Not To Impress

In my past 25 years as a motivational speaker, to the best of my knowledge, approximately 4.5 million people have heard the message of my story. Perhaps you are one of those who happened to buy this book from a news-stand, or at one of our seminars or corporate conventions, we may not have even met but I hope this story will inspire you just as much as it did the others.

Yes, my first objective is to ensure that this story inspires you. It is not my intention to impress you with the things I have accomplished. And frankly, there is no need to. I believe the way to motivate someone is to show him your way to riches, not to show him your wealth.

Be Tough Too

It is a tough world. I started this book with this chapter. 'Life Is Tough'. The intention is to magnify the true essence of life; *life is tough, life is not easy.* Knowing this truth about life, I guess we need to be a lot tougher with ourselves so that life can be easier with us later. This is my second objective in sharing my story.

Several years ago, I had the opportunity to meet Dr Robert Schuller, in California. He is a dynamic pastor and the founder of the Crystal Cathedral in Garden Grove in California. His famous quotes.

Tough times don't last, but tough people do

People with paper qualifications have a better start in life than those without them. I had never felt the importance of paper qualifications until my recent meeting with Professor Dr Deric N. Bercham, from New Zealand. He is the Chancellor of Bercham International University. He and Professor David Chu from Taiwan have made me realise the importance of education. I was their guest at a graduation ceremony held in Subang Jaya in 2001. There were about 60 graduates in the processional march, the ceremony was grand, there was so much energy in the grand hall, each one of the graduates was thrilled, their faces were radiant with pride. Yes, these are some of the people I know who have sacrificed so much in their pursuit of educational excellence, for they know the importance of it.

Empathy

My final objective in sharing my story with you is to tell you that whatever feelings of fear, rejection or hopelessness you may have, I too, know these feelings, I too, have walked in your shoes before. I empathise with you.

I understand the feeling of fear, of reaching into my pocket and not finding any money there. And I understand the feeling of avoiding the landlady because the room rent hasn't been paid for the past three months.

I understand the frustration of self-pity because I have stood in front of a food-stall, starving, hoping to meet someone who will buy me a meal for another day.

I understand the feelings of fear, anxiety and worry. Yes, I have been there before. You are not alone.

Here's my story...

I was born in the year 1953, in a remote little town called Melaka. I spent my first two weeks in a maternity hospital there. My mother had put me up for sale. Word got around that there was a baby boy for sale, and a lady from Port Dickson, Negri Sembilan, came to investigate. She saw me for the first time, and she asked, "How much?"

The nurse replied, "The baby's mother wants $1,200"

"$800, take it or leave it...After all, we are not rich people, talk to the mother, please," the lady told the nurse.

The sale was concluded at $800 and I went home to Port Dickson with this lady, Teh Kian. My new mother. She didn't have a husband, and I grew up without knowing what a father could provide. I never knew who my real mother was or where she was. To me, that's irrelevant. My life took shape with my new mother, Teh Kian.

This is Kian Seng, my brother

I have a brother and a sister, both much older than I. Our lives depended upon the income from a fruit-stall operated by my mother. My mother was a thrifty lady, saving was an essential to everyone at home. We were taught about the value of money right from a very young age.

My mother enrolled me in a Chinese school in Port Dickson. I walked to school daily wearing a pair of worn-out shoes. My classes started in the morning and by 2.00 pm I was back home. By the age of nine, I was already out in the streets, selling ice-cream. Everyone in the family was expected to manage, struggle and help out. Daily, I would rush home from school, change my clothes and walk over to the ice-cream manufacturer to pick up my ice cream flask and ply the streets in that little town. The memory of those joyful days still dazzles me for it was the first time I had earned money. On the good days, when I managed to sell all the ice-cream in the flask, my income would be around $1.00-1.20. Normally, I would hand over all the money to my mother. It was simple work, unimportant now, yet it was a beginning which left an indelible mark on my mind.

You will agree with me that there is normally, for everyone, one place that one frequents, where one enjoys oneself, or finds comfort and sometimes opportunity. Whether you are in business, sales or still in school, there is always a favourite place or 'joint' to go to. My 'joint', at the age of nine was the theatre. It was known as Seaview Theatre (it has since been demolished to give way to development). As an ice-cream boy, just like many others of today, one of my privileges was to get into the theatre without having to buy a ticket. Before the show started, I would mingle with the crowds outside the theatre. Sometimes, I would go into the theatre earlier to serve the early patrons. Normally, by the end of the show, I would have sold every stick of ice cream. But, if sometimes I felt that business was not doing well in the theatre, I would stroll down to the beach or to the harbour and approach the picnickers and fishermen.

There was this unique incident that I have never forgotten. One afternoon, as usual, I was in the theatre, selling ice-cream. On that particular afternoon, 'business' wasn't going as planned. Only a few of the patrons were willing to buy the ice-cream. So I strolled down towards the harbour area. After hanging out there for half an hour or so, screaming at the top of my lungs "Ice-cream, ice-cream," I couldn't find any prospective ice-cream lovers. My instinct told me that I should head back to the theatre.

By the time I got into the theatre, the show had begun and it was dark, so I began groping in the dark. While waiting for my eyesight to get adjusted to the dark, I began my 'business.'

"Ice-cream! Ice-cream! Ice-cream!" I shouted in the middle of the show. I was frustrated at getting no response from the patrons, so, I raised the volume of my voice and again shouted, ice-cream! Ice-cream! ice-cream!

The annoyed patrons shouted back, "Shut up!"

I was frightened. Afraid that I would be barred from the theatre forever, I kept very still for a moment. Noticing an empty seat, I sat down and watched the entire show. At the end of the movie, just like everyone else, I came out of the theatre. Only then did I notice that something was wrong. The lid of the ice-cream flask was missing and naturally all the ice-cream had melted. Remember, we are talking about the sixties when air-conditioning was not a feature in the theatre. When the melted ice-cream was returned to the manufacturer, the manager who ran the shop wasn't quite convinced with my story. He took the ice-cream flask and went on his bicycle to my mother's stall.

"Auntie, we have entrusted the ice-cream to your son, but he returned with this...," complained the manager, as he showed the lidless flask to my mother. She didn't argue with him. She just paid for those unsold ice-cream sticks floating in the flask.

The demanding manager left our stall. I was angry, humiliated, and at a loss. I was cursing the manager. My mother who heard every curse, looked at me and then taught me my very first lesson in life. "Son, if you wish to work for someone, say good things about him. If you want to curse him, quit! Then you can curse all you want!" she said. Naturally, I was not able to accept her theory at that time. Then she concluded by saying, "Besides that, you must remember, that when you are given a job to do, do it well. If a man pays you a dollar for a job, do a three-dollar job."

WHEN YOU ARE PAID A DOLLAR FOR A JOB, DO A THREE-DOLLAR JOB

Growing up in that little town was boring. In fact, not many things interested me. I was mischievous, in and out of trouble all the time. I must admit that I was not a good kid. One day, I overheard a neighbour telling her children not mix around with me too much, "That boy is a bad influence, he is always getting into some kind of trouble...Stay away from him." Despite the fact that my mother tried her best to discipline me whenever she could, it did not have much effect. She was at the same time trying her best to ensure that her family could survive decently on the meagre income from the fruit stall. Occasionally, she would break down in tears during one of her lectures to me, "Why don't you give it a rest, son. Grow up, for goodness sake, I am almost out of my wits trying to ensure we have meals on the table." Then, I would please her, and behave the way she would want me to...for about...three or four days.

For a long time, I had suspected that something was wrong with me, but just couldn't figure out what was actually wrong. One day, I overheard my mother telling her friend at the kitchen table, "I think something is wrong with my boy."

"What's wrong, Kian?" her friend asked.

"I notice he is so different from your son. You see, whenever, my son opens his school books, his eyes automatically shut, and when the book is shut, his eyes are wide open. Whereas your son is doing it the right way," my mother concluded.

As far as I can remember, and as far as the school records show, the only time I was in the A class was when I was in

Standard One in Chung Hwa Primary School in Port Dickson. And for the rest of the years in the primary school, I was in either C or D class. No one told me the importance of education, and school homework was never supervised. I guess some of the teachers had also given up on me. The only joy in going to school was being able to hang around with my classmates.

Years went by. Soon the day came when I was filled with doubt as well as happiness. I was transferred to an English school. I am sure many of us have been through that particular feeling when we were transferred to a new school. Seeing new faces, listening to a new language and checking the notice board to find out which class I was assigned to, I managed, somehow to pass the first day in a new school. The year was 1966.

God was with me, I knew that deep within, for when I was transferred to the new school I was put into an A class. Many of my ex-classmates from the Chinese primary school were put into H or J class. I kind of missed them. There were unfamiliar faces all around me and almost everyone spoke in English. Many of the students seemed very confident. As usual, I was seated at the back of the class, timid, quiet and fearful. But, day by day, my confidence grew. I began to make new friends, some of them were really helpful. No one ever turned to me for help in school homework; I was the one who made them feel important.

The following year, my aspiration became a reality. I was put back with my classmates once again in Form One I. I felt at home with them. Then came Form Two I in 1968, and the following year, Form Three I. Suddenly, I became aware that I was in a very 'dangerous' year, a compulsory year of the Government Examination which must be held for every Form Three student. If you fail this examination, then that's the end – dropout!

To cut the story short, I failed along with some of my 'good' friends. "Why have you failed in your L.C.E. examination?" my brother asked.

I didn't dare tell him the reason, but deep inside, I knew it was due to all the fun, fun and lots of fun of the past four years in my Secondary school.

AS YOU SOW, SO SHALL YOU REAP

I blame no one. I had failed the examination. I deserved it. I should have done what I was supposed to do—study, I should have concentrated on studies instead of running around, clowning and wasting my life. I accept the verdict.

AT THE END OF THE DAY
I HAVE TO ANSWER
FOR MY OWN ACTIONS

I could not possibly go to the Headmaster (HM) and beg for sympathy, ask him to let me through to Form Four. Can you imagine me saying this, " HM, please let me through, I promise you that I will study hard the following year." Similarly, a farmer can't go to the paddy field and beg God to give him a good harvest if he does not toil for it.

This is a law which we shall call the Universal Law of Nature. You reap what you sow. Very similar to the law of gravity. The law doesn't care if you believe it or not, it works all the time.

Whatever you want in life, LABOUR for it. Nothing happens by accident. If you want better grades in your studies, spend more hours studying at home or in the libraries.

If you want more sales, make more sales call. First sit down, make more calls for appointments, confirm the appointments, GO and SEE each and every one of them. (If you don't call them, they won't call you!)

If you want to be a millionaire, learn to save and invest!

If you want anything, ask for it. I hope you still remember the preface, our Kenny's story. God wants you to be successful, for He created the birds, and the worms. But He certainly didn't make those worms appear beside those birds – even the birds have to fly out from their nests…to look for worms. Similarly, you need to put in more action in order to get the results you want.

Discontented, Discouraged But Determined

At 17, I was still a naïve young lad. However, I was willing to take a chance on anything that could bring me instant success.

So, I went out searching, and only then I was told by an old man, that there is no such thing as instant success, "Forget it, David! There is no such thing as instant success!"

Since then, I have long forgotten about the idea of instant success in life.

Discontented, discouraged but very determined, I decided not to go back to school. It was time for me to look for a job. I had the certificate in my hand, but I decided to hide it somewhere, afraid to look at it, and worse still, what if someone else were to see it? After all, the certificate was of no help to me. What could I possibly do? With my lack of education, who would want to employ me? These questions flashed across my mind.

"Go and look for a job!" my mother told me. I spent weeks of wandering around the streets. I would leave home early and return late at night, and hope my mother had gone off to sleep, to avoid her long lectures. Finally, I found a job that needed little or no tertiary background, a job as a worker at a construction site.

My first three friends in my working life

THE WORLD GIVES

EXACTLY

THE SAME AMOUNT

OF OPPORTUNITY

TO EVERYONE, SEEK IT.

THERE IS

NO

INSTANT SUCCESS!

My first job was as an unskilled, under-aged and under-paid labourer in a construction firm in Port Dickson. I began work at 8.00 am and got off at 5.00 pm. All day, I worked under the hot sun, and digging drain, unloading bricks from trucks, mixing cement, sand and aggregates to make concrete, or the easier work would be watering the turf, all for $1.50 a day.

I remember there were days when I was taken to a remote place where I had to work, all by myself. Digging trenches for pipe-laying purposes. The contractor would buy me a pack of rice for lunch, and someone would pick me up at the end of the day.

"What did you do all day long? You have hardly dug up 10 feet of the trench, you stupid idiot. Have you been sleeping on the job? What are you good for anyway? Can't you do something without being supervised for once? And what am I going to tell the boss? Idiot!" The supervisor would verbally hassle me for a while.

"That's what you get for $1.50 pal…" I would feel like saying to him, totally ignoring what my mother had taught me right at the beginning. However, I remained silent and accepted the intimidation and humiliation, I knew I was being exploited but I had to start somewhere. Months went by…

One day, while working in another place, still digging trenches, and unloading bricks from trucks, a man approached me.

"Aren't you David Goh?", he asked.

"Yep! That's me." I looked up at him, holding a spade in my hand.

"You shouldn't be working here David, you are wasting your talent. I have seen you in one of your school concerts. You can sing very well, why don't you come with me to

Seremban? There is a band that needs a singer, I think I can convince the band manager to hire you. Stop wasting your life here David," the man advised.

Early in 1971, I began my second career as a singer in a band. We called ourselves the Evergreen. I was paid $50 a month, with a commission of $25 per engagement. Everything was paid for, food and accommodation, and most of all, I enjoyed the work. The band lasted about nine months after

As a singer with Evergreen

which the band manager decided to fold up the business because he wasn't getting enough engagements to keep all the members going. The expenses exceeded the income. Evergreen became 'Evergone' in a short time. Soon after that I found myself back at Port Dickson. By this time, my elder brother, Kian Seng, had ventured into construction, so I went to work with him for $3.50 a day as a general worker.

Working with my brother was a lot tougher than working for the previous contractor. My work involved working as a general worker during the day and guarding the site store at night. I literally lived at the construction site for a year and a half. My brother (who died of heart-attack in 1987) was a tough man. He would stretch me to full capacity, making a young boy work like a man.

I have never forgotten a certain bitter experience while working for him. It was a hot, sunny day, with a clear, blue sky, not a cloud in sight. I was told to go to a new site. It was a site for a new housing estate. My assignment was to dig trenches for laying concrete beams. There were lots of planks with rusty nails everywhere. Carelessly, I stepped on one of those planks. I didn't know it until a rusty nail burst and went into my foot right through my shoe. The other workers came and gave me one of the oldest and most effective treatments to ensure that the foot does not get infected. First, they pulled out the nail from my foot, and then they slapped the wound with my shoe until the blood was oozing profusely, and then wiped it clean. Next was the tough part; they then poured some match-powder over the wound, and lit a match. "That will do it! You will be all right," they said to me and indicated that I should rest nearby. Carefully, I sat down, so as to not injure my foot further. After about twenty minutes or so, I saw my brother's car approaching the site. He got down from the car, came up to me and said, "Why are you resting here while the rest are working? You are my own kin, and if you are just sitting around instead of working, the rest of the workers will follow your example. Don't set a bad example..." His voice was stern.

"I had injured my foot..." looking up at him, I explained.

"Instead of sitting down not doing anything, why don't you pull out those used nails from the planks, and recycle them. I am sure your arms are still working..." he ordered.

DISCIPLINE IS TO TEACH

Some of the skilled workers advised him, "Boss, you don't have to work the boy out!" They sympathised with me. My brother, as tough as ever, told them, "I am not raising a building, I am raising a young man." He was tough! Oh, how I hated him at that moment, but if he had been kind, good and overly concerned about me, I would not have learned from that bitter experience.

Come to think of it, God had a plan for me. I am being positive. He wanted me to walk the rugged path and taste the bitterness of life before I could enjoy the reward of success.

In reality, one would not need to walk the rugged, difficult path if one had only planned ahead. If early foundations are laid, then the structure of success can be erected without many auxiliaries. As a speaker and trainer, I have met so many CEOs in the industry, who earn over RM500,000 per annum. Many of them started out as an executive somewhere, but most of them have high tertiary education. There are some exceptions to the rule; some of them had no back-up of paper qualifications, they really had to go through the grind to reach the top. These are people who toiled for decades in order to reach the top positions. Is education important? Of course!

I was never happy during my days as a construction site worker. It was a tough life. I was looked down upon, had been turned way and talked at. There were times I wished I had not been born. Many times I cursed the situation in my life. There was a time when I was asked to go to an engineer's house to work in their posh residence. When we (a skilled labourer and I) got there, we were told where to get the water and where we were to mix the concrete. I remember the lady of the house came out and said, "Work in the designated areas and don't come over to this side of the house…" she indicated the patio, and turned and walked away as though she was talking to two criminals. I wanted to leave there and then.

WITHOUT PAIN,

THERE'S NO JOY

WITHOUT EXPERIENCING

BITTERNESS

YOU WILL NEVER KNOW

SWEETNESS

"This is the way the rich talk to the poor, lad, she means no harm," my skilled friend assured me.

At home, I was treated more or less similarly. I was the black sheep of the family. Since they seemed to hate the sight of me, I took the liberty of staying out and there, another problem arose.

It led to my getting mixed up with the wrong company and returning home late in the night. To me, staying with the family was like a solitary confinement, but with very little income, I couldn't stay on my own. So, I stayed on at home. Mom had given up on me, she often said to me, "I wonder why I took the trouble to adopt you in the first place..." I could sense her disappointment, but I was really helpless...and hopeless, but I was unable to do much.

Gradually, I got tuned to believing that the world was rotten, and that to be rich one had to be a crook, that rich people were not nice people. I learned to blame others for my own mistakes and failures. I learned to take short-cuts in everything I did. And worst of all, I began to think that God was dead, and He was not helping me in any way. Evidently, I was wrong.

My brother was doing well in his construction business. Sometimes, he would take all the workers out for lunch, and I had the opportunity to go along. Eating good food in posh restaurants and enjoying myself for a short time in an air-conditioned environment was comforting. "Now, this is luxury..." silently, I envied him.

I yearned for the good life, wanting to break free from home. " I will never be able to make it if I stay back in this town...got to get out of here. Got to get away from the bad company I am mixing with. Moreover, I need to be independent," I said to myself. In 1972, through a family friend, I was recommended for a job in Port Klang.

"What's the job?" I asked this family friend.

"Tally clerk," he answered.

"A clerk," I thought to myself, "wow, this is going to be a big break in my life, and when I make it well, at least my family members will bother to give me a second look, and I will not have to face another day of rejection and humiliation. My thoughts were improving.

After packing some clothes, I went to bed early. I wanted to face the morning sun as soon as possible. The next day, I left for Port Klang. True enough, the job was waiting for me.

The title 'tally clerk' may seem prestigious, but the work was tough. Every day, about 35 tally clerks came for the job, but only 10 were hired. In other words, we were virtually picked for the job day by day.

If you were close to the supervisor, or the store manager, you had a better chance of being picked for the job. The walk, from where I stayed to the office, took 40 minutes, so in order to ensure that I was picked for the day, I had to begin my day as early as 6.00 am.

Working hours were from 7.00 am to 7.00 pm.

Naturally, the old timers were the ones who got to work 20 days in a month. The newcomers like myself got only 7-10 days work in a month. The pay per day was $10. Generally, I was paid between $65-$125 a month. The room rent cost me $60 per month, and the balance $5 had to last me for at least 10 to 15 days, otherwise, I would have to resort to other means like borrowing money from friends.

When the reality strikes you, you realise that life is tough, it ain't easy. But the tougher you are with yourself, the easier life will be later on. Staying on your own feels great but for everything else too, you are on your own. Although there is no one to look over your shoulder, there is also no one to look after you.

When you do not have enough money for food, let alone to buy a bar of soap for your bath, the soap powder from the nearby washing machine suffices. How would you like to live in a rented room where the light bulb is only of 10 watts (dim)? "If you wish to bring in an electric fan, I will have to raise the rent to $70," the landlady had forewarned. My landlady was unique. She would stand outside the bathroom door and count the number of buckets of water you used. If you used more than 10 buckets of water, she would wail, "Don't waste too much water!" Boy, what a degrading way to live!

There were times when I was so broke, I could afford only a 20-cent plate of rice with curry. Most of my personal belongings, like my guitar, Amco jeans, hockey stick and badminton racket were sold in order to keep me afloat for another month. Experiencing these setbacks, I thought of packing up and moving back to Port Dickson where everything was provided for, but the thought of facing those who had looked down on me prevented me from doing so. And today, I am glad I stayed back and went through those days of hardship. It proved to be a rich experience.

My Self Image Improved

While working as a tally clerk in Port Klang, although I had to face hardship, and some unpleasant events, my self-image grew silently within. I began to think like a clerk, the image of me as a school dropout no longer existed in my mind. My values grew bigger and stronger. For the first time in my life, I found myself much worthier than the time I spent in Port Dickson.

Dr. Napoleon Hill says that *"thoughts are things which when mixed with a definite purpose, persistence and desire, become a powerful tool to attain anything one wishes."*

During the entire episode of my stay in Port Klang, I began seeing the 'clerk' within me. Dr. Maxwell Maltz, the late plastic surgeon and author of *Psycho Cybernetics* has said: *If you desire to achieve a bigger and stronger self-image, then actively think about being a winner in life. In whatever situation you may be, think like a winner."*

I believe there is a reason for our existence. I really believe that you and I are not in the world by accident, but for a specific objective. You need to believe in yourself, and the good Lord wants you to be successful.

In the past decades, so many students have come and gone in our classes. I have had the opportunity to talk to ex-convicts who have made good of their lives, I have students who came to my seminars in wheelchairs, on crutches, and some blind students were there too. I must say their aspirations in life were high and their determination strong. These people were so focussed in their search for success that they would put an average person to shame. In one of my books, *Effective Sponsoring Skills*, I have mentioned the names of many people who have made good of their lives despite their handicaps. I have had the opportunity to meet and talk to many such people.

As a matter of fact, most of them started changing their lives only when they began to believe in themselves. A few of them testified that the moment they began to think they could make it, almost automatically their confidence in themselves deepened. They threw away the belief that they were destined to be poor and their lives destined to be handicapped.

One of the most interesting things that happened to me was that when I started to communicate with the officers in a shipping company, I was able to relate to most of them, thus giving my self-confidence a boost.

Unlike the time when the lady of the house treated me like a condemned convict – my self image was so dismal then. Most of all, I began to see myself in a more positive manner, as a worthier person. I am grateful for that job as a tally clerk and to the people who gave me another chance to improve myself while I was there.

3

The Importance of Strong Self-Esteem

Too many people fail because they feel they should fail. They don't believe they have the right to succeed. They are self-destructive. Exercise the right to be successful, because this is your God-given right. The right to succeed. Unfortunately, our school system does not teach the student the importance of living a life with strong self-esteem. On many occasions, when I have been invited to universities, both in Malaysia and overseas, to discuss the subject of self-esteem development, these activities were organised by the students themselves. Strong self-esteem is so important that it has a direct impact on our lives.

Each day when you wake up in the morning and look at yourself in the mirror, ask yourself a few questions:

How do you view yourself this day? Important? Or do you feel like an unshaven bum?

How do you look at your own world?

As big, happy and challenging? Or simply as a small, sad and pathetic world?

What will this day bring you?

Frustration or challenges?

Frankly, the answer lies within you. They are dependent upon what you feel about yourself.

Another term for self-esteem is self-image. It has three components and they are very important. My entire life changed, because of this self-esteem.

First Component: How you feel about what you do, determines much of how you feel about yourself. In other words, if you feel good about the job you are doing, the chances are that you feel good about yourself. How many times have we had this experience? I am sure on numerous occasions you have been given an important task for the next day. It could be a day when you will be out accompanying a guest from overseas, or simply attending an association meeting with the CEOs, because your boss told you to take his place for the day. The excitement you feel is indescribable. The next day, you wake up with a great feeling. And may be for once in your life, you look forward to doing something so important.

Second component: How you feel about yourself is the image that determines how effectively you will work. You feel good about yourself, knowing that someone like your boss has faith in you that you can do the job. Naturally, you expect yourself to be effective.

Third component: How effectively you work determines how much you will earn. This is the end result of what self-esteem is all about. Being effective. You should be rewarded for the effectiveness in you.

Start today, get a new mental picture of yourself. Begin seeing the qualities in yourself. Start by seeing the goodness. Powerful self-esteem is one of the most important and basic qualities of a winner. The feelings within you will tell you your own worth. Start bragging a little about yourself. This exercise does not require a basic degree or Ph.D. It is so easily done, just by turning on your own projector hidden within you. Allow your subconscious mind to go to work for you. Many call this auto-suggestion. It is a process that leads to a better quality of life.

BEGIN TODAY,

SEE A BETTER PERSON

IN YOURSELF

GIVE YOURSELF A TREAT,

REWARD YOURSELF

BECAUSE YOU ARE

SO SPECIAL

Warning: When I say start bragging a little about yourself, it means just a little. This is a grey area, where most people have the tendency to cross over, and then they are termed as egoists. Brag a little. When you brag too much, you turn everybody off, you may offend others.

Self-esteem is about feeling good about yourself and not about satisfying your ego all the time.

High Self-Esteem vs Low Self-Esteem

If I were to skip this page, I would not be doing justice to my readers. I think it is very important that you are given an insight into these characteristics of self-esteem. Let's look at a list of ten points of high and low self-esteem. Go through the list, you may find it very interesting.

Sl. No.	High Self-Esteem	Low Self-Esteem
1	tends to look directly at the person he/she is speaking to makes eye contact	does the opposite avoid eye contact
2	does not raise his/her voice confident that he/she can be heard.	speaks very loudly desperate to be heard
3	wears clothes that are appropriate for the occasion and are comfortable	wears clothes to impress others all the time, even if they are uncomfortable
4	does not brag presents facts that may sometime reveal some of his background	brags to impress makes up stories to project a stronger self-image thereby hiding his true weakness
5	is not afraid of being alone	is afraid of being alone and needs someone all the time
6	presents facts	distorts truths
7	lives in the real world	lives in a pretentious world
8	takes responsibility does not blame others when things go wrong	does not take responsibility blame others for his failures and frustrations
9	feels happy when someone else do well	looks out for others to fall and fail in life
10	is generous to others	is jealous of others

I would like to add that one should aspire to have the ability to adopt all the ten qualities or characteristics presented above. They are very much like the Ten Commandments in the Bible. It is very hard to follow all the commandments. However, I would like to encourage you to acquire as many as you can, but if you can't live up to all ten, don't be discouraged. After all, we are only humans, aren't we? It is easy for me to present these facts to you, but to follow them takes a lot of sacrifice. Frankly, I have never come across anyone in my life who has acquired all the above ten qualities. Only a perfect human being can do so, isn't it?

Live your life to the fullest and live it with strong self-esteem. Strong self-esteem pays. When you increase your level of self-esteem, you automatically expand your perimeter of capabilities and beliefs.

Don't live in the shadow of yourself, reach out for growth and new personal adventures. While it is easy to live within our own comfort zone, we seldom want to try new things, exploring new limits and expanding our boundaries. If you desire to grow and achieve new levels of accomplishment in life, you have to believe that you have virtually no limitations except those that you choose to place on yourself. Frankly, the only time you reach the limit of your potential is when you choose to go no further.

Two local authors have written about this subject and I suggest you read them. One of the books, written by Poh Teck Lim, a Master of Business Administration from Durham University, U.K, is *Mindful Challenges Towards Peak Performance*. Poh and I have worked together on several occasions, and you will enjoy his presentation.

The other is Ranjit Singh, who co-authored with Jack Canfields the book *Self-Esteem*. Both these men started their careers as professional speakers. They are very experienced and authorities in their fields. If you have an opportunity to listen to them, I am sure you will get a deeper insight and understanding of what I have mentioned in this chapter.

There are some immediate steps that can help you develop stronger self-esteem without regard for sex, creed, colour, religion or circumstances. These 10 steps will transform you into a better individual and allow you to experience a better life.

10 STEPS OF TRANSFORMATION

Step # 1

Get Involved In Public Speaking

It is a well-known fact that one of the greatest fears in the world is speaking in front of a group of people. I have been involved in this field for the past twenty-five years, and I know for a fact that public speaking promotes greater and stronger self-esteem. When you are asked to speak in front of a group of people, you will then begin to think, "I must have something special to share, otherwise, I wouldn't have been picked for this occasion." With that initial thought, your self-esteem grows.

Step # 2

Rich Projector

Starting today, begin to put in a new picture of yourself in the rich projector within you. It is important that you put in a happy, successful and rich person in this rich projector. Next, spend 10–15 minutes daily watching this new picture of yourself. It is an antidote for belittling, self-destructiveness, and other negative elements.

Step # 3

Read Autobiographies

Reading is a habit you need to develop if you want to progress in life. Once you develop this habit, then, you need to read autobiographies. One of the surprising things I learnt when reading autobiographies was that people without much tertiary education went on to build empires of their own. The wealth they accumulated was enormous. When you read books like this, you begin to think: if this person can do it, so can I. That's what healthy self-esteem does to your thinking.

Step # 4

Take-Twenty

Every day, spend twenty minutes at mid-day to relax. Do nothing except relax. In this process, you will find that you rejuvenate and revitalise your level of thinking. It is a mind-control relaxation time. You can do it by sitting down, or simply lying on the floor in your office during lunch hour. All it takes is 20 minutes. If you can turn on some calm, soothing music to complement the atmosphere, it will be an added benefit. When you are revitalised, your self-esteem is also enhanced.

Step # 5

Motivational Cassettes

Conrad Hilton, the man behind Hilton International once said, "Not a single person should go back without listening to those motivational messages. I have plenty of those cassettes in my car, at home and at the office."

In recent years, bookstores in Malaysia have been displaying dozens of motivational cassettes. Listening to these messages daily will definitely give you a lift. Motivational cassette listening was one of the ways that I had applied in my life-changing experience. And till this day, I still crave for it, every other day. When you are motivated, you can't feel small, because your mind is geared to a task. It is good for your self-esteem.

Step # 6

Mentor's Corner

Why do you think there are so many Kodak cameras being sold in the country? The answer is obvious, people like to remember every occasion, be it an important personal one or a moment with a celebrity or your mentor...someone important. Every once in a while, there comes a moment in life when we get the chance to stand next to a well-known personality for a photo opportunity. Remember, we treasure such a moment, it is a moment we are proud of, and most of all, it is a moment when our self-esteem gets enhanced.

It is with this intention that I wish to point out that a mentor's corner must be created in your home. In the past, we have moved home several times. And each time we moved,

I would first identify which wall in our house would be the mentor's corner. There, on the wall, I would arrange these framed pictures of my mentors. And pictures of me with other personalities are also neatly arranged.

One of the secrets of this mentor's corner is that it strengthens your self-esteem. Remember, anything that makes you feel good, that lifts your spirits is good for your self-esteem. A mentor's corner is a memory of your past happiness, a moment of pride in the past. Remind yourself that you have come this far, you have met some of these personalities who have faith in you, who believe you. They are your motivation. Sometimes, when things go wrong, sometimes when things are slow, and when you are down, go to the mentor's corner and get charged up again.

Step # 7

Past Victories

Very seldom do we write down our own credentials, unless we are applying for a job. Credential writing is a healthy exercise. It may be half a page, full page or several pages. It comprises your past victories. Learn to write down your own past victories, it is another way to strengthen your self-esteem. Memorise your past victories, read those credentials several times, until they get firmly fixed into your head.

Step # 8

Dress Well

There is a correct dress code for every occasion. I believe we need to dress well for all occasions. I have told you earlier in the chapter that we do not need dress to impress others, but we need to dress comfortably, and I would add dress comfortably and well. When you dress well, you talk well, you behave well, and you think well. I would like to share one

of my experiences with you. Writing – as an author of many books, writing has become a major part of my life. Members of my family understand the importance of my writing, they know that nothing must come in my way when I am writing, and they leave me alone. When I am writing, I dress neatly and comfortably. I think well, and I am focussed, because I start at 4.30 in the morning and spend an average of 10 hours in front of my computer screen daily if I am on a tight schedule to complete the book. I must be focussed, and I have found that dressing well helps me tremendously in this area.

Step # 9

Brainwash Yourself To The Top

Brainwashing was a technique used by the Red Army that once dominated our country. The first Prime Minister, Tunku Abdul Rahman, was faced with this and, he knew that if he did not act quickly, his entire effort in bringing independence to the country would be wasted by the Red Army. Yes, brainwashing is that powerful and effective. Using the same technique, I brainwash myself to climb out of the valley of despair and desperation. Using a good message or slogan that will enhance your self-esteem will do the job. This is the line I used : "I am getting better and better, every day in every way!"

Step # 10

Exercise Daily

I play golf these days, and spend some healthy hours sweating it out. I swim with my children whenever we have an opportunity. I know the importance of exercise, and I make sure I don't exert too much. Several years ago, when we were living close to a gym. Judy and I would spend 3–4 hours each day at the gym. We seldom got sick and seldom complained about backaches or shoulder stress. However, when we moved to a new place, and could not go to the gym for exercise, backaches, and shoulder stress became common complaints.

Now, Judy and I play golf, we are back on track. When you feel healthy, you feel good, and when you feel good, your self-esteem automatically goes up.

Development of self-esteem is critical for anyone who wishes to get ahead in life, who wants further personal progress. It doesn't matter what you do for a living. You can be a clerk, or an office boy, an executive, a supervisor in a factory, or a salesperson selling toothpicks, a manager in an almost-out-of-business enterprise or self-employed.

Everyone will get an equal chance to grow and progress if only they can further enhance their self-esteem. This is the first and most critical step one should take.

I have seen and talked to a waiter who later turned into a successful businessman. I also have known and witnessed a bell boy turned taxi-driver and then subsequently, owner of a car hiring service. I have seen and spoken to an office boy who became a salesperson, and then went on to become a sales director in a public-listed company.

You don't have to go too far, just go to any direct selling company or life insurance company. There you will get to see a number of people who once didn't know what to do and where to go and then became household names in their trade. How did they do it?

Easy. It all begins with stronger self-esteem. They believe they have been created for a special reason, and most of all, they believe that they can achieve anything they want if they believe in themselves a little more.

First it is the belief in oneself, then in God, and then in the product one sells.

Do things go wrong with you sometimes? I am sure everyone has been through such things. Do you feel that you are sometimes driven away from your goals, something that your heart desires, you are not getting near it, as a matter of fact, you are being driven further away. Sometimes, it seems you can't make progress, and there are obstacles everywhere. Have you had that feeling?

If you have, then welcome to life. That's life. In life we are faced with insurmountable challenges, with image of failures that block your path to success.

What do you do in such situations?

Well, what I am about to tell you may seem like an easy task, but living through it will be uphill. However, I must also

tell you, no motivator any where in the world, can give you a guarantee that when you do what you are told to do by them, you will be a success.

Trust your instinct. Believe in yourself, learn to believe in these words:

"This day shall pass...I am strong, and I will not let this day destroy me. This day shall pass." Trust in the good Lord, that He is there to hold you in times of trouble. I am a Christian, and I am taught to believe that He who made the world will ensure His children are safe and well. I trust Him just like you should trust your own religion and your creator to protect you and guide you. Remember, when your siblings are about to get into trouble, you run to help, don't you? That's the same belief I have and you should too. Don't spend too much time worrying. Worry is a sickness that haunts you night and day. It robs you of your happiness. Steals away your good times. And separates you and your beliefs. It is about something that has not yet happened, so, why do people spend all their lives worrying about something that has yet to happen. I don't get it

SELF - LIMITATION

IS ONLY

A

STATE OF MIND

4

The Road to Discovery

I spent a year working as a tally clerk in Port Klang. I made some new friends, and then I left the town for home with some pretty good memories. The job was not getting me anywhere financially, I was flat broke, no more than just surviving, although the job gave me good exposure.

As I mentioned earlier, then I began to see myself as a much worthier person, thinking and acting like one. I no longer saw myself as a Form Three drop-out. My self-esteem grew tremendously in that one year. All that time I communicated in English with people in Port Klang. I have some good friends who were kind enough to correct me when I mispronounced some words. Reading the English newspaper aloud was a great help. On the other hand I was also mocked by critics on several occasions when I didn't speak English so well. With each cynical laugh, I was more determined to improve myself.

A friend recommended that I work in the city of Kuala Lumpur. That was in late 1973. The night before I left for Kuala Lumpur, my mother spoke to me: "Son, I believe you can make it in life, I don't know when, and I really don't know how you would do it, but I believe in you. Do the best you can!" With that she put a $100 bill in my hand. "I really can't afford much, let this $100 be a start," she said.

I was to work as a labourer initially at a construction site earning RM5.00 daily. If you remember, in the 70s, the room rental in Kuala Lumpur was around $150-180 that my pay was barely enough for. A simple meal cost $2 per day. How was I to afford these luxuries? What could I do in order to survive in the city? The $100 from my mother was not much of a guiding light either.

Improvising on the Situation

Once in a while, we will all be faced with difficult situations in life. Some may be easy to sort out, and some may be very complicated, and take years to sort out. However, it is important that we figure out a way, instead of running away, that we stay on and try to figure out a way – I call this improvising on the situation.

As you can see, I was in a situation then, how could I survive in a city with just $150? I had two choices. The first was, I could pack up and crawl back home where my needs would be shamelessly taken care of. Or the other, I make do with what I had and go on from there.

"I need to fight this one out…" I thought to myself.

So, I asked my boss if I could stay at the construction site and help to look after the machinery and materials. "We have got a night guard to look after the site, why would I need you to look after the place?" My boss was not a very friendly person.

"Listen boss, two guards are better than one, after all it will cost you nothing," I assured him. He figured that it was a good idea, and he agreed. Hence, my lodging problem was solved.

My first few months in the city of Kuala Lumpur weren't easy. Sleeping at night in the middle of the city in a construction site office was not easy. The noise, mosquitoes, dust, and dirt—combination of stress. And having a bath at a site office can be quite an experience, while passers-by look at you strangely. The construction site where I was working is today the building that stands proudly, diagonally opposite the Pudu city main bus terminal – Bangunan Cahaya. The bathroom then was a temporary make-shift one for general workers to take a 'leak'. It was a cubicle made of three zinc sheets, with a broken door. Can you imagine taking a bath with hundreds of people passing by the construction site? Some would stop to investigate. There was no time to think of anything else at that time of my life, I was a plain labourer making a living. Was it a difficult situation? I guess you can call it one, but at that point of time, I didn't see it as a situation. As a matter of fact, I was actually glad that I had a job and a place to live. I wasn't contented but I was a 21-year-old young man learning to survive in a big city…with a faint vision that one day I could make it. However, I was glad to be working in a big city.

I remember the evening of 15 September 1974. Alone at the construction site—the security guard was patrolling at the far side—I sat outside the construction office. The entire place was dark except for the fluorescent lighting from the temporary office. I sat there in the dark with only the mosquitoes for company. Memories of the good times with my friends in Port Dickson and in Port Klang, and the forever-cherished moments with mom at home in Port Dickson came flashing back to me.

"Why am I so lonely at this moment? Where are all my friends now?" I was lonely. I felt that I should shut my mind off and not continue with this unhealthy, trip of self pity. I stood up and walked out of the site. I wanted to change the view.

"May be I should go and have a drink, I thought."

My hand reached into my pocket, and could only come up with $1.35 cents. Afraid that I would spend all the money and would have to starve tomorrow. I decided to watch the passing cars, and the people walking the streets. Everyone was going somewhere. Some still in their office attire, others dressed casually, a few of them well dressed.

I could tell some had just come from shopping, from the way they were struggling with those bags loaded with things. There were beautiful and fancy cars everywhere, big and small ones, all of them a fabulous sight. The city neon lights were relentlessly blinking away even at this time of the night.

"Will I ever own a car one day or a house may be…?" I wondered, then I thought, I can't afford to even rent a room at this point of time, let alone owning a house. I was unclear about my future, and many questions raced through my mind on that night of September 15th, my 21st birthday.

"Everyone is entitled to a big celebration on his or her 21st birthday and should be with their family members, but why am I left without a friend in this crowded city alone?" I was lonely. I looked up at the night sky, it was filled with stars. There were these three stars, neatly arranged in a straight line, which I had seen and talked to many times when I was so much younger.

"Is this the life you had promised me?" I spoke to those three stars as if I was talking to God.

"No, I am not through here! I want to and I will, make it in this city! If I need to find a way, you have to guide me then…" I murmured under my breath. I must have gone to sleep late in the night because very soon I was awakened rudely by a loud honk and seconds later, there was a knock on the office door.

"Hello! Hello!" someone called out.

I peeped through the window and saw a huge truck full of cement bags.

"Cement, cement!" the man howled, indicating that the ordered cement had arrived, and he was awaiting further instructions to unload.

"OK, I am coming." I glanced at the office clock, it was 7.05 am. I stretched out my arms and I yawned. I knew it was time to go down to help unload those 200 bags of cement into the store room.

That was it. My simple 21st birthday celebration was finally over.

By 1975, I was forced to abandon my 'home-office' (office cum home) because I was transferred to another site. My boss had offered me a permanent job – as a storekeeper at $240 a month. With that pay I could afford to rent a room for $100 some 15 miles away from where I worked. I was proud of the

Me with the vibrating Machine

A picture to remember my construction days in KL

Bank Rakyat in progress

fact that I was able to have a room to myself, storing my personal belongings, unlike the time when I had to sleep at the site office of Cahaya Suria where the office table was turned into a bed at night, and the telephone directory become a pillow, where clothing had to be tightly, hurriedly tucked away for fear of discovery and reprimand by the bosses.

At the new site, I was given more responsibilities, besides being the storekeeper, I was also in charge of keeping the record of workers on the various floors. It was a bank taking shape – the Bank Rakyat in Jalan Tangsi.

That year went by rather quickly. I was enjoying my days in the city. Making new friends as I went along. Many of them were in sales and some of them worked in factories. I envied those working in factories, "I am on the night shift, that's why I am able to come and visit you at the site, David," one of them claimed.

"How much do you earn working in a factory?" I asked enthusiastically.

"$900 is my basic, sometimes, with an allowance of $250 I usually take home slightly over $1000 after tax and EPF," my friend would brag a little.

"Wow, over $1000 a month..." I thought to myself. Thinking of what I could do with that kind of money, I envied my friend more.

"Why don't you try selling? The career of a salesman isn't so bad, David." Some of them genuinely encouraged me.

"I don't think I am cut out to be a salesman, I can't talk well, and don't know how," I was honest with my answer. However, I chose to shut my own door, so my friend didn't pursue it.

Only on the alternate weekends (Sunday), I got a day to rest, and normally, I would go to be with my mother. She was beginning to have more confidence in her 'prodigal son'. We spent countless hours together. She would cook the meals I loved to eat, reminding me of the love she once had for me.

In June 1975, I was on the 30th floor of the building, overseeing some workers clearing debris in the area. A friend of mine, Ronnie Yu, got permission to come up to visit me. "They told me you are here. So, I came," he said as he glanced out of the building. "Wow, the view from here is magnificent! Looking at the entire city from here is unbelievable!" he said.

The view from the 30th floor of the building had no impact on me during those days, I saw it all the time. " What brings you here anyway, Ronnie?" I asked.

"Listen, David. Why don't you come with me this Thursday to the Equatorial Hotel. A very good opportunity has just arisen. It could be the turning point in your life." No one had ever said such words to me, and it sure sounded morally uplifting.

"What is it all about?" I asked Ronnie

" Don't ask further, all I can say is that you will not regret it," he said enthusiastically.

Ronnie Yu was probably two years older than I. Good looking, and a fast talker. He thought fast, and was always on the alert. He was a very successful salesman, selling corrugated boards for a local company. My boss had hired his company to supply those boards about a year ago, and that's where I met him, and we became friends. He was always very encouraging. And I liked hanging around with him.

The much awaited Thursday finally came. That evening, Ronnie came to fetch me at the site in his new Alpha Romeo. I felt a little uncomfortable because of my attire, a short sleeved shirt, with a button missing, and untidy-looking long pants without a belt, while he wore a jacket that looked like a politician's.

I could smell the cologne the moment I entered his car.

My shoes were, of course, a disgrace, mud-stained all over, and I was very careful not to dirty his car.

"I am sorry for the mess," I told my friend apologetically.

"Don't worry David. You didn't have time to go back to freshen up. I understand," he assured me.

We arrived at the hotel at about 6.00 pm. "We have an hour or so. We are early, let's eat something here," Ronnie told me.

"Here? Ronnie I can't afford eating here. I have never been to this hotel before, and..." I said.

" Don't worry David, I am buying," he interrupted.

I liked Ronnie's life style. Dining at the finest restaurant, driving a fancy car, wearing an expensive outfit. How I would daydream that one day I would be like Ronnie Yu. I even tried calling myself Ronnie Goh instead of David Goh on one occasion. It doesn't sound right, I told myself. I tried to emulate Ronnie in so many ways, and frankly, I just couldn't catch up with him.

We went into a hall after our dinner at the restaurant. Some people in the room instantly recognised Ronnie. " Good to see you here Ronnie," a few of them walked up to him and greeted him.

"This is my friend, David," Ronnie introduced me to them.

"Welcome to the party." Their responses were warm, and I felt so wanted. Nobody seemed to notice my shoes and my attire. I was so ashamed of it, but there was nowhere to hide. Somehow, I knew there were some people who had looked at me strangely.

"Let's grab a drink," Ronnie told me.

While chatting with Ronnie and a few of his friends, the music in the hall suddenly faded away. Then one of the organisers went up on the stage, behind a rostrum.

"Welcome, ladies and gentlemen. Shall we take our seats?

I can see many of you have invited some of your friends along. Could you please introduce them?" the man said. With this, Ronnie turned to me, and said "Would you like to stand up and introduce yourself, David?" I looked at him in disbelief. "Are you kidding?" Ronnie, then helped me to get introduced to the group.

Later that evening, I discovered that the meeting was a gathering for all the part-time sales people for *Time Magazine*. They were on a recruiting drive, and that's how Ronnie ended up inviting me there. The following week, Ronnie came to the site and helped me to register with the company as a part-time salesman.

A New Trade Means New Opportunity

Learning a new trade, selling wasn't an easy task. I had a mental block. Right from the beginning, I didn't like selling as a profession. I had never considered that I would one day be a salesman. It remained a job until I discovered the joy of selling.

The fallacy I had was that a salesman needs to be a good talker – Wrong!

He needs to walk from one house to another, knocking on doors – Right then! (Now wrong, because selling is about networking today.)

He needs to learn to talk fast in order to be evasive – Wrong!

He needs to be able to twist and turn – Wrong!

He needs to wear a long-sleeved shirt with a tie – Right!

He needs to cheat, lie and bluff his way through –Wrong!

He needs to beg, and beg and beg again –Wrong!

Only the desperate will eventually get this job –Wrong!

However, when I went through the training, I discovered many things that enabled me to make a good living in this profession of selling. Gerry Hawthorn, a sales trainer, was engaged to train us, the part-timers. He said something that I will never forget, "This is a new trade for you and it means a new opportunity. This is a second chance in life for you to make good financially." In four days, we were given product knowledge, and taught the basic selling skills. After which we were given the green light to go out to make a living with this new skill.

Ever since I got involved with *Time Magazine*, every day became a brand new day for me; the days became brighter and a ray of hope shone in me. Every day at 5.00 pm, I would rush from the site to the *Time Magazine* office, do some planning, then join the others and hit the road, knocking on doors. By the time we (part-timers) met at a designated place, it would be around 10.30 pm, after which we had dinner. It was a nightly affair for six days a week. Sunday was optional. We could either choose to rest or join a group of other salespeople combing a housing estate, knocking on doors, promoting *Time Magazine*.

Some of us became more enterprising; we improvised on the system by buying some cheap stuff from wholesalers to be given as premium gifts. Knocking on doors, ringing people's door bells, and when the owner of the house peeped out, "auntie or uncle, I am from *Time Magazine*, our company is giving away this premium gift to the house owners in this estate, no obligation..." we would raise our voices hoping that, across the driveway, the other auntie would take notice.

One day, a very unusual incident took place. I would like to put it on record, as it may be fun to share it with you.

One evening, I was out in a housing estate promoting the magazine as usual. I took out a torchlight key-chain and, dangling it in my hand, I rang the door bell.

A man came out and he asked, "What do you want?"

"Sir, I am from *Time Magazine* and my company is giving

away this torchlight key-chain," I said. "Here..." shining the torchlight and indicating to him to come out and get it.

" Hold on," he said as he shut the door.

I stood there by his front gate and waited for him in the dark. Minutes went by, the mosquitoes were getting increasingly unmanageable, but not wanting to be rude, I kept waiting. I glanced at my watch, couldn't see how long I had been waiting, then I pressed the door bell again; no one came out. I waited for another minute or so, then pressed the door bell again, again, no one came out.

All of a sudden a vicious-looking dog came charging towards the gate where I was standing. It scared the daylights out of me. Fortunately, I was outside the gate. The man came out again, and this time he shouted, "Now, if you still don't get the message, I shall open the gate. Get the hell off my place!" I could only walk away with humiliation. A few paces later, I heard a lady's voice behind me.

"Come back here." It was a lady standing behind the gate now instead of the dog. "Young man, my husband means no harm." She tried to unlatch the gate, and I shouted, "Wait, wait, wait..."

"What?" she asked in surprise.

"Your dog..." indicating that her dog could mean a lot more harm than her husband.

"Oh, don't worry, it's been tied up." She assured me.

"Wait, wait, wait..." I screamed

"Now what, young man?" she asked again.

"Your husband..." I turned and ran for my life, because I could see her husband running after me with a baseball bat.

I didn't close any sale that evening, When we all gathered at the designated place, where we exchanged our stories and experiences, I told them my story, and one of them stood up and suggested that we go over to the house again and beat up that man. We laughed, and left it at that.

Sure, a salesperson's job is full of an amazing number of funny, horrifying, sometimes serious, but most of the time satisfactory, experiences.

There were a lot of challenges given to the salespeople by *Time Magazine*. I won most of them. The first one was for a trip to attend the Asia Time Sales Conference in Rasa Sayang Resort in Penang. It was a three-day affair and those who qualified would travel in style – by plane. I had never stayed in a hotel and never been on a plane before. The motivation was great. I went all out to ensure success. The campaign took us three months and I succeeded within two months, ahead of the others. The sales conference was a great help to me. My experiences were shared with others in the region. And subsequently, I won more and more awards and trips.

Word got around that I was a good, useful salesman. Offers came pouring in from various organisations. One company offered me a permanent job as their salesman, with a basic salary of $300. I didn't take that offer and instead I stayed back with the construction company and resumed my part-time activities with other direct selling companies. I sold cosmetics, imported sheepskins, car accessories, perfumes, and cookware. Learning how to demonstrate the cooking utensils took a lot of skill. Steaming a fish, cooking a pot of rice and steaming a plate of vegetables within 15 minutes was all so amazing to the ladies for whom I demonstrated the use of my set of pots and pans. I sold hundreds of sets monthly. Earned a good income and saved enough to invest in a car, which would come in handy as I travelled around with sets of cookware instead of one set at a time, I thought. So I bought my first car, an obsolete model of the Austin 1100, worth $2,800 and spent $3,000 on repairs. I spent more time repairing the car than driving it around...I think. I decided to sell it, and finally sold it after trying to do so for 19 months for just $1,500. Actually, I was glad to get back $1,500 for it.

I was diligent in my work at the construction company and my boss treated me fairly. My salary went up to $380 in 1976. With the income from my part-time sales, I was able to change to a better car which was of great help in my part-time selling career. On some weekends, I would drive to another town to sell the pots and pans.

I remember it was one of those weekends when one of the supervisors in the cosmetic company came to me and said, "David, if you can hit next month's target, you will be able to win yourself a ticket to attend a motivational talk by Malaysia's top motivator." Frankly, I didn't even understand what the term 'motivation' meant, let alone talk about attending the seminar. However, I knew what hitting the target was all about, and I loved to take on those challenges, "OK, consider it done!" I told Mary, the supervisor. And true to my expectation, I hit the target and got myself the ticket.

The talk was on a Tuesday evening at the grand ballroom at the Hilton. There were probably 1,000 people there. And I was seated in the middle of the hall, together with Mary and a few other cosmetics consultants. The speaker was a short, Malay man, named Mohammed Isa. He was a very powerful speaker which naturally caught my attention.

By 10.30 pm, when the talk was over, Mary asked me if I would like to have a word with Mohammed Isa personally. I said, "Sure!" Later, Mary told me that there was another seminar which I could attend. It was to be conducted by Isa himself.

"It will be held in early 1977, you can register for it," she told me.

"How much is the investment?" I asked her

"$350 per head." Wow, one month's pay, I thought to myself. Anyway, I paid for it and waited for February 1977, when I attended the two-day seminar. It proved to be the turning point in my life.

It was a personal development workshop, and Isa had done a great job in providing the training. I have never forgotten what Isa said, "What determines your success is your attitude. Start right and act right with a positive mental attitude." I learnt about setting a goal and reaching the goal. At the same time, I was inspired by Isa to speak in public. So, towards the end of 1977, I spoke for the first time in my life in a club. It was short, and simple…Yet it was my beginning. With that first experience under my belt, I took up public speaking as a hobby. There were so many free speeches I gave in that year alone.

My First Book…

Now I know why there are so many people who don't pick up a book to read. It's the first book that leaves a lasting impression, be it interesting or boring, or simply too confusing. If one picks an interesting book, that is easy read, then there is a continuation of reading, and the habit would be formed. If one picks a boring book and it is too confusing to begin with, after a few pages, one will just dump the book aside and generalise that books are boring, and the habit of reading will not be formed.

My first book happened to be interesting, and reading it was easy. It was during the time I was speaking in public. I needed to expand my knowledge in this area, and was told that self-help books would help me. So, I began to develop the habit of reading and collecting motivational books. The first book that landed in my hand was the book written by Og Mandino, *The Greatest Miracle*.

Ronnie Yu, who was about to leave for the UK, came to

the site one evening just as I was packing up to leave for home.

"Hi, what brought you here at this hour?" I asked Ronnie.

"David I came to bid you good-bye, my family and I will be leaving for the UK next Saturday." he said. I felt sad because I knew deep within me I was going to miss him.

"Here, let me give you this book as a present." And he placed Og Mandino's book in my hand.

"Good luck to you David, and good bye..." he shook my hand with great warmth.

"Good bye, and I thank you Ronnie for everything you have done. I will always remember you and cherish the moments we had together." I wasn't good at saying good bye, and wasn't good at hiding my emotions. "Will I ever get to see you again?" like a young lad, I asked.

"Maybe...who knows?" Ronnie said.

I shook his hand for the last time. He turned and left the construction site office, and that was the last time I met Ronnie Yu.

The book was left in my car's glove compartment, and I had totally forgotten about it till one Sunday, while I was cleaning the car, I came across the book again.

That night, I sat by my kitchen table and read the first few pages. It was easy reading, and I just kept on reading. By the time I had completed half the book, it was well past 2.30 am. I never felt tired, the book just kept me going.

A few days later, I had finished reading the book.

Then someone called me on the phone and asked if I knew about Og Mandino's book, entitled *The Greatest Miracle*. Once again I picked up the book and read it again, and then again. I must admit, Og Mandino's *The Greatest Miracle* was one of the earliest books that had helped shape and change me into what I am today. I wrote to him, and never expected him to reply. However, a month later, I received his reply, and till this day, that letter is still in one of my speaker's files.

I made a pledge after the last time I read *The Greatest Miracle*. I would like to meet Og Mandino. It was a simple pledge, and it took me five years to realise it. In 1982, I met up with Og Mandino for the first time, and through his coaching and mentoring, I learned many wonderful skills to be a writer.

Books. Can one do without them? I really don't think so. Since then, books have been a constant companion to me. As Charlie Jones, an associate speaker and a friend has often said, "Depending on the books you read and the people you mix with, you will never be the same in five years' time." I urge you to pick up a self-help book today, and even though it may seem dull in the first few pages, try to be persistent, read further, you will find it interesting. I sincerely believe that no author in this world will write garbage, and even if they do, no publisher would want to publish it.

So, if you want to progress, begin with one of the cheapest ways—reading self-help books. I am going to take this opportunity to advertise the books I have written which I would highly recommend you buy.

The Making of a Super Salesperson
Blueprint For Greater Success
Step Into The Future With Nothing (The Day The Eagle Took Off)
Start Selling, Stop Order Taking
52 Ways to Make More Money in Network Marketing
Effective Sponsoring Skills
Making a Career
40 Reasons Why You Lost That Sales
Here's How You Can Speak Better
Secrets of A Top Sales Performer
From Zero to Millions – The LKH Story

To Be A Professional Speaker

THE RIGHT BOOKS

YOU READ AND

THE RIGHT PEOPLE

YOU MIX WITH

WILL GET YOU

ON THE ROAD

TO

EVERLASTING SUCCESS

I wake up at 5.00 am everyday, read a chapter or two that gives me a lift inspirationally before I go to work. I prospect for people to book me to speak instead of buying my cookware. Most weekends I get to speak before groups of people. Thus, I gain confidence as well as experience.

One day, I was invited by a good friend, Victor Lee, to speak to his group of sales people. "David, we are organising a sales conference in Fraser's Hill, and I would really like you to join us, you could come as my guest, and give my boys a motivational talk. But bear in mind, I don't have a budget for your professional fee. Would you like to come along?" He asked. I took up the offer without a second thought.

I Did It My Way

The day came. Victor came to pick me up. It was a pleasant journey I remember. " So, you are going ahead with this career in full steam David?" Victor was in a jovial mood.

"There is no turning back, Victor," I assured him.

We talked about everything. Our ambitions, life and other successful speakers we knew. Finally, we arrived at the then Merlin Hotel where we were staying. The rest of the participants were staying in a bungalow and all of them were packed in that six-room bungalow. That was the first time I was treated like a speaker.

"If you wish to order anything, just go ahead David. Everything is on the house," Victor said to me.

I felt good, and my self-esteem increased a little from that day onwards. When night came, I excused myself and retired early, because I wanted to be fresh for the next day's seminar. Before I slept that night, I remember I said a little prayer, asking the Lord to give me the inspiration and wisdom to perform my very best the next day.

The morning call was right on target - 6.00 am. "Good morning Mr Goh, 6.00 am, this is your morning call." The

receptionist was polite, and I felt extremely good. Never in my life had I been treated with so much courtesy.

I met Victor for breakfast at 7.00 am at the coffee shop. "Did you sleep well?" he asked.

"Never like this before, thank you Victor," I responded.

By 8.15 am, one by one, the participants arrived at the hotel, and by 8.45 am all of them assembled in the hall. That day, I did it my way. I gave a talk that would leave a lifetime impression. I was good, and I knew I was good because Victor came up to me when the seminar was over at noon, shook my hand, and said, "That was great. David, you were terrific!" He gently put an envelope in my hand, and sensing that he didn't want the others to see, I excused myself and headed for the men's room.

Alone in the men's room, I opened my hand to see what it was. It was a red envelope (ang-pow) which contained a $50 bill and a note from Victor.

It wasn't the money that made me cry with joy, it was the note Victor had written: David, may be this is the beginning

of your speaking career, keep it going, signed Victor.

With those few lines, Victor gave me so much of encouragement, and by 1978, I knew the time had come. I went to my boss in the construction company, and told him that I wanted to resign.

"What do you plan to do David?" my boss asked.

"I want to be a professional speaker," I said.

"You want to be what?" He quipped.

"A professional speaker." I said firmly again. And took some time to explain what professional speaking is all about and how I could make a living doing it. After much persuasion, my boss stood up and patted me on my back and said, "I think you can…" With that we shook hands, and that was final.

My desire and ambition to be one of the best speakers in the country were building up. I was becoming very determined.

"Look David, I don't mean to put you down. There are so many other speakers in this city, they are big boys in the industry, they will not give you a chance to be in this game. Don't be foolish by quitting your job," a 'good' friend advised me. "Besides, do you have anything worthwhile to speak on, would people want to pay to listen to you, really I don't think you should go ahead with this idea. I care for you, that's why I am advising you. I hope you don't take it another way." He continued with his 'words of wisdom'. But my will and desire were building up, and my mind was made up. This 'good' friend could go to hell for all I cared, but the speaking industry was where I was heading. And nobody would come in my way.

I am afraid in our society today, we have many people who are jealous of other people's success. The things they say are

ADVICE IS THE

CHEAPEST COMMODITY,

YOUR 'GOOD' FRIENDS

WILL GIVE IT

WITHOUT YOUR ASKING.

FOLLOW YOUR INSTINCTS!

AND BELIEVE IN YOURSELF

of value to others and in reality they only portray their own sense of insecurity. These are people who will put you down, and always be there to condemn and criticise everything you try doing or have done. If you fail, they will come along and say, "I told you so, didn't I?" And if you succeed, they will avoid you or in case you do meet up, they will say, "Some people are born lucky."

What do you do with such people? Ignore them. Once you have made up your mind, go ahead as planned. Who are these people to tell you how to run your life? Where were they when you needed help? And did they really help even when they were around?

Think about it, if at all, you are the only one who is answerable for your actions. Not your neighbour, your classmates, teachers, not even your parents. Essentially, it is your life that you are trying to mould to become a better you, and not theirs. So, why should they have a say in it? We are living in a new millennium, gone are the days when we needed to refer to our neighbours for a decision to be made. Today, society is so advanced, and with the progress and advancement in information technology, parents today are trying hard to match their children's mentality, let alone teaching their children about empowerment. However, I can understand that not all parents are like that. Some parents are so domineering, they like to control, and are abusive in many ways. Living with parents like this can be very strenuous. Growth, I am afraid is restricted, and progress is limited as well. But nonetheless, one day, these people (parents) however bad or good they are, they will have to go, and when they are gone, ask yourself a question: where do you stand?

Wouldn't you agree with me that many people who aren't successful, both financially and also in their own personal happiness, were once actually controlled by parents or members of their family? They were once controlled and conditioned to think "safe".

They were repeatedly told not to do this , not to do that. So much so, these 'safe but destructive' affirmations were drummed into them to mould them into what they are today – very safe. Their thinking perimeter does not permit them to think further than their daily routine.

I began charging a professional fee of $150 for half a day's talk. This went on for a few months in 1978. I couldn't come up with a one-day talk, because of the lack of material.

Then things began to take a down turn, people were not booking as much as I had expected. I hardly got a paid engagement for a few months. I was struggling, and to some extent a little scared. Not knowing what was going to happen the next day, and how I was going to continue... Should I go back to my boss in the construction company, I asked myself. Then I warned myself, "David , if you go back to him, your entire dream of becoming a professional speaker would be gone!" I struggled on.

Months passed. It was November 1978. A company that I had some dealing with during the construction days came to my aid. The CEO was an Australian, and he gave me an opportunity to speak to his executives and managers for $500. And once again, my confidence grew. At the same time, I was promoting Mohammed Isa as my other speaker, and with my ability to organise, I began to earn some side income as an organiser for other speakers. That kept me going.

1979 was a great year. The first quarter was full of activities. Several companies asked for my services, and time really went by fast. Soon, I was running around all over the country.

Local newspapers were writing articles about me, and bookings were coming. However, towards the last quarter of 1979, things slowed down again. For almost four months, I went around trying to figure out how to go on with this business of mine. It was a test of time. Things were really slow, but I had no room for giving up or giving in, so I persisted. Days turned into weeks, and slowly, the months went by.

"David, I would like you to read this book," Mohammed Isa gave me a book which looked to me like a mini telephone directory.

It was *See You At The Top*, a book written by Zig Ziglar. I took it with a smile and a 'thank you.'

I went home that night, and started reading the book. It was another self-help book that left a lasting impression on me, and I made a pledge to meet up with Zig Ziglar one day. Then, I wrote to him, to express my gratitude, thanking him for providing such a wonderful book that helped change people's thinking. I was not expecting it, but a reply came. And subsequently, I wrote to many authors who later became good friends.

Almost five months went by without any bookings coming in. I was broke, and frightened. Then came the first month of 1980, I was forced to sell my car, to take off the financial pressure from my shoulders. However, I was still persistent, and I knew deep inside, that the tough time would surely pass, I just needed to get through this impasse.

In March 1980, I was booked by a direct selling company to train their distributors throughout the country. "This is too good to be true." I said to myself. The contract for the entire year was for $75,000. To be honest, I have never had such major success before. The client was kind enough to place a deposit of $15,000. That gave me some breathing space.

First things first, I went to buy myself a car, and the rest of the money, I invested in a low-cost house, which had only two rooms. Nothing fancy, but it was my first house. The year went by so wonderfully, working with the distributors, helping them in their sponsoring effort. Travelling with the

A TEST OF TIME

WILL EVENTUALLY

BRING OUT

THE BEST

WITHIN YOU

distributors was an experience. Training the distributors from town to town was very challenging. Bit by bit, I was gaining a lot of knowledge in managing a direct selling company. Working with the management, and understanding how they work gave me better insight to the trade. I worked very hard, and I gave more than I received. The company was very happy with my performance. One incident which I will never forget is the time when we were in Penang and we had scheduled to train the distributors in Johor Baru, the southern part of Malaysia, the following morning at 9.00 am. We expected 75 participants in the class.

We didn't turn up on time the next day, because the car driven by one of the distributors had engine trouble. No one came to help, so we slept in the car that night. There were five of us sleeping in the troubled Toyota Corolla. When we were rudely awakened by some people knocking on the window, I glanced at my wrist watch, it showed 3.50am. Who could it be at this time of night? I wondered not sensing that we were about to get into trouble. One of the distributors said, "Don't open the door, and don't wind down the window." With our silence, the three intruders became more unruly. They began kicking the car, trying to smash the windscreen with their bare hands. We were terribly frightened. Then one distributor said calmly, "don't panic, keep calm. They are only three of them, whereas we are five, we can easily overpower them, or at least talk some sense into them." We all agreed, and the next thing I knew we were rushing out of the car as though it was on fire. By the time we got out of the car, the three men sensing that we were desperately defending ourselves, panicked and ran down the road, never to come back. We stood there, shocked and angry! We spent the entire night talking, laughing, not wanting to go back to sleep for fear those three men might return. When daylight came, we were exhausted. A taxi came our way, and took one of the distributors to the nearest mechanic. Half an hour later, the distributor came back with the mechanic, who was able to get the engine restarted.

We called the hotel to inform them of the delay. By the time, the car got fixed, it was already 9.30 am. And by the time we got to Johor Baru, it was nearly noon. We somehow managed to get all the 75 distributors back to the class after lunch.

What does this lesson teach? Never try to work on a tight schedule. And when travelling, always ensure the car is in tip-top condition.

I have thought about it a thousand times. What if the three men had carried weapons? What would have happened to all of us? The incident is now just a memory of the past, however, it was through such experiences that I became the David Goh of today.

At the end of 1980, I met up with Dottie Walters, Ed Foreman, Art Fettig, and Charlie Jones in a national conference held in Malaysia. Dottie Walters told me about the National Speakers Association in the USA. "David, if you really want to grow as a speaker, let me introduce you into our association," she said. "And you should go to their convention to get to know how these professionals work..." she continued.

In 1981, my application was approved by the National Speakers Association in the USA, and I was pronounced a professional speaker. With my application approved, my self-worth jumped. So did my professional fee.

I began to charge $1000 for half a day's speech. 1981 was a good year, I had almost 48 bookings in the year, worth $80,000, not to mention the contract I had with the other direct selling company which was worth a lot of money. My perseverance had finally paid off. My immediate goal was to get to the USA, attend the National Speakers Association convention. The trip would not come cheap, so I had to begin saving for it.

USA Here I Come

Living on a low budget, I managed to save $17,500 in a short span of time. Finally, the day came. USA, here I come. The flight to Los Angeles took approximately 20 hours. I was glad that Dottie and her husband, Bob were at the airport to welcome me. I lived with them for a week, visited Disneyland and places I had seen only on TV.

Everything looked new to me. One evening, as I sat on

the patio in Dottie's house, I looked back at the changes that had taken place in that short span of time. I was glad that I had resigned from the construction company, and taken control of my life at the age of 25. "Had I stayed back and played safe, I wouldn't have landed in this great land of opportunity – the USA," I thought to myself.

After a week, I took a flight from Los Angeles to New York and met up with another speaker. I was introduced to many wonderful people in the speaking industry in a small gathering at a hotel there. I spent a week in New York, where getting around was not a problem for me at all. In that short time, I managed to get in touch with the late Dr Norman Vincent Peale, the author of *The Power of Positive Thinking*. We spent an afternoon at his office and from him, I learned many interesting things, from writing to speaking on the platform, from religion to positive thinking. Time went by quickly, and my one week was up. Then I flew off to Phoenix, Arizona, where I was to attend the National Speakers Association convention. Sommers White, another great speaker from Phoenix, was at the airport to greet me. He helped me to check into the hotel where the convention was being held.

One thing led to another. Finally, the moment came, when I met up with the man who wrote *The Greatest Miracle*, Og Mandino.

The Thing You Least Expect Comes With Big Surprises

"I wrote you a letter some years ago. This book has been with me for more than six years, I have read it so many times, and it has certainly helped change my life, Mr. Mandino, I would like you to autograph it for me." I said to him.

While he was autographing the book he said, "I do remember you, David. You are from Malaysia." I felt honoured that he remembered me. I observed him, and thought to myself, "Wow, if only I could write a book…"

Meeting up with Zig Ziglar was another great experience. I was in the foyer, gathering some information from a few other speakers, when someone whispered that Zig Ziglar and his wife had just walked. He was like a star, a celebrity. Then I saw a few people rushing up to him with his book, asking for it to be autographed. I made my way through to him, and

I was sure that being the only Chinese in the crowd, Zig couldn't miss me. As I walked toward him, he looked at me smiled, and I introduced myself, "Hi, my name is David Goh, from Malaysia. I wrote you a letter a few years ago." We shook hands. " Hi, David. Welcome to the USA. Dottie told me about you earlier, is this your first trip to the USA?" The conversation went on for a few minutes, it was effortless, and motivating. Spent a short time with Zig, but the motivating effect was evidently deep.

The week spent at the convention was worth it. When it was all over, I flew to Dallas, Texas to attend Zig Ziglar's course. And then went to St. Louis to attend a Positive Thinking Rally where Zig was the headline speaker. Later, I came back to Dallas to spend another five days with Ed Foreman and Earlene Vinning, both speakers from the Executive Development System, who gave me a tour of the city of Dallas, and we ended the evening by going to the movie, E.T.

A few days later, I was in their four-day workshop, "Life is Terrific".

"David, I really think you should attend Tom Hopkins' class. Since you have so much experience in selling and have won so many outstanding awards in this very field. Tom is a champion salesman," Patrick O'Dooley, one of Ed Foreman's team members, told me. I agreed. He helped me enroll in Tom Hopkins' class in Houston, Texas. A three-day sales training that gave me a totally new horizon. As you can see, the thing we least expect may come up with big surprises. It all began with a desire to meet these people, then I wrote them letters to express my desire. I left it at that, never expected them to reply, but the end result was all a big, pleasant surprise!

At the end of 1981, I telephoned Og Mandino at his home in Arizona, and expressed my interest in writing a book. He gave a few tips, and told me to attend his mentoring programme the following year. "I am scheduled to touch on the subject of book writing, you should be in that class, David," Og mentioned.

With the basic tips and guidance from Og Mandino, I went to work on my first book, *The Golden Path of Success*. It was a simple book that spelled out some principles and my struggle in making good in life.

I sent the manuscript to a few local publishers, but all of them returned it, saying that they were not interested in representing me.

What could I do? So, I had to take the bull by its horns, take the lead myself. I got it edited by a school teacher (despite her major in English, there were so many mistakes!) typeset and had the printer print out 5,000 copies .With these, I went out to the market selling it as my own product. Selling my book from platform to platform was exciting. Soon, the 5,000 copies were sold and I had to reprint another 5,000. "Shouldn't you go for 10,000 instead of 5,000? It would be so much cheaper than to run only 5,000," the printer tried to convince me.

"OK, let's make it 10,000 then," I said, after calculating the difference in price. I must admit, the book managed to help me out financially.

Enthusiasm Makes The Difference

The month away in the USA did me a world of good. I was refreshed and rejuvenated. I was like a child who had just stepped into Disneyland for the first time in his life. All excited. Then, I began to work on my two and three-day seminars. After that I started marketing the seminars. At the same time, I initiated the first Positive Thinking Rally in the city of Kuala Lumpur. It was a huge success, more than 800 people turned up for the event. And, subsequently 13 other Positive Thinking Rallies were held in this city.

Enthusiasm makes the difference. Every day, I woke up

with a great feeling. I was enthused, and went out there to market my seminars diligently. While going about with my business, I gathered enough material to come up with my first sales programme, titled. Sales Orientation & Leadership Development (S.O.L.D.) It was an instant success with several sales organisations. The programme took me to Indonesia, Hong Kong and the Philippines. The more I went to the market, the more enthusiasm I developed. There was enthusiasm in both my voice and action. The people around me imbibed so much of my attitude, they too, could not help but feel enthused as well.

I waited for June 1982 to come. Again, I went to the USA to meet up with the professionals. Obediently, I enrolled in Og Mandino's class on book writing. As I handed my book, *The Golden Path of Success* to him in the class, he shook my

hand and said, "Congratulations, David, you did a fine job! This is fabulous." Og Mandino turned to the class and told them how an Asian like myself had taken the first steps to begin writing a book.

"Fear is the key that prevents a lot of potential writers

from writing. They are so worried about people laughing at their mistakes, and about rejection," he told us.

When I came back, I started working on another two books. *Achievement Through Superpower* and *Ray of Light*. Again, the local publishers weren't convinced of my potential, they rejected my manuscripts. So, I did what I had to do. Took the lead myself and when that was done, I had a whole warehouse of books to sell.

Through 1983-1985, I was doing more sales training than motivation. Since the development of the Sales Orientation & Leadership Development (SOLD) seminar, I had been busy with the sales training workshops for major organisations in and outside the country. The sales training programme was introduced to various companies in the Philippines, and, subsequently, I was invited to conduct a similar programme for several organisations in the USA. While in the USA, I came in contact with Dana Corporation Inc, in New York, where I spent substantial time. Dana Corporation had more than 35,000 distributors all across the US, and my job was to provide the motivation the distributors required, so I was literally hopping from one state to another. That event gave more depth to my understanding of multi-level-marketing and its operations. At the end of 1985, I met up with the President of Forever Living Products Inc., in Arizona. With his introduction, and a warm handshake, I was engaged in 1986 by his company to provide training to their branches in Malaysia and Singapore which weren't doing well. I spent one full year with them, working very hard, sleeping in hotels more often than at home. I managed to help turn around the ailing branches from a monthly sales turnover of RM25,000 to one of RM1.2 million. With this outstanding result, my credentials increased considerably.

In 1985, Jim Harvey, an American whom I had met during

SUCCESS COMES WITH

THE RIGHT NETWORK

THE RIGHT NETWORK

BEGINS WITH

A WARM HANDSHAKE

one of my previous trips to the USA, talked to me. "David, I have a proposition to make." That short conversation led to the setting up of David Goh International and Jim Harvey & Goh in Australia. Jim moved to Australia, where he spent the next 15 years, marketing my seminars and representing me worldwide.

A very creative and hard-working marketing genius, Jim worked to sell me and my services to clients in different parts of the world. And he did a great job. We had seven staff members working for us. I invested a large amount of money in setting up the office in Australia. Working with Jim is like having your father working in your office. You leave almost everything to him. Jim knows what to do and who to contact. "My job is to get you up there speaking. Your job is to do it well," that was his bottom line.

The Australian operations opened up a new horizon. True to his word, Jim got me to several parts of the world to share the platform with some of the very best. The income rose year by year, and the staff were given an annual tour as an incentive. "David, let's work toward the USA," Jim said to me while we were having lunch one day at an exclusive restaurant in George Street in the city of Sydney. I agreed, and Jim began to put his network together.

Meanwhile, back in Malaysia, most direct selling companies had heard of me, and the services I provided. I began to spend more and more time in this area. I was often booked by these companies at their conventions, as a keynote or headline speaker.

My SOLD programme was marketed to various companies in Malaysia. In 1986, Singer Sewing Machine Company got in touch with me, and the first SOLD programme was conducted for a group of 60 sales agents. They all learned new skills in their sales approach, and then the

Sales Director, Woo Heng Choon, instructed that the entire sales force of agents must go though the SOLD programme. More than 6,000 sales agents and the entire management staff went through my sales and motivation workshop. It took me a year and four months to complete the assignment. By the time I had completed the Singer project, I was 34 years old. I did about 500 programmes that year alone. And in the same year, my 'dream' of a house with a swimming pool, was realised.

When I appeared in the Singer International Convention

as their headline motivational speaker, word got around that I was the one responsible for the excellent training provided to the sales agents; and dealers from different parts of the world began to contact me to train their sales agents. With that introduction, I got to travel to many parts of the world.

EVERY NEW VENTURE,

BE IT GOOD OR BAD

OPENS UP ANOTHER HORIZON

OF UNLIMITED POTENTIAL

AND OPPORTUNITY

IF ONLY ONE CAN

SEE IT!

My Dream Fulfilled

It was a Saturday morning in June 1988 when the telephone rang in my hotel room. It was the wake-up call from the reception at the Hilton Hotel in Kuala Lumpur. Minutes later, my breakfast was brought to the room. I sat down to eat and, looking out of the window, I had a clear view of the then Kuala Lumpur racecourse. It's a beautiful day, I thought to myself. I tried recalling the time when I had just arrived in the city. How much misery I had endured. It had taken me so many years to turn my life around. Many events occured, some not worth thinking about, while many others were exciting. Making my dreams come true was an uphill task. Yes, I realised that my first million would get spent fast if I wasn't careful with my expenditure. Making the first million is the toughest, as you may have heard, and how true that was. Sitting there, watching the world go by from the hotel room at the Hilton gave me a comfortable feeling, a feeling of contentment yet, I knew that there was no stopping…

Some Dreadful Events

Meanwhile, in the same year, my brother Kian Seng's construction company had landed him further in financial problems. He struggled to get out of them, but the more he tried, the worse the situation became.

Trying desperately to salvage whatever he could from a bankruptcy lawsuit, working and living in great distress and under tremendous stress, Kian Seng just couldn't stand the pressure, he was broke, and finally, he called me,

"David, I need to get out of town for a short holiday, could you loan me RM500?" I sensed a quiver in his voice.

"For you anything, my brother! I don't have to loan it you, I will be glad to give it to you. I will send the driver to give you the money," I assured him. Kian Seng and I never had a good relationship when we were younger, and working with him was hell, as you may have realised in the beginning of this book. However, I thought this was a good opportunity for me to repair the damaged relationship. I gave him RM1000 instead. He was happy that I was able to help out. My mother was happy as well. Needless to say, I was the happiest of them all.

When Kian Seng came back from the short holiday, it didn't seem to have done him any good, and a short time after that...I remember it was sometime in June 1987, I was on my way back from the southern part of the country, I had to pass through my hometown in order to get back to my home in Kuala Lumpur.

I had a sudden urge to stop by at my brother's house. So, I asked the driver to drive up to his house. As we were approaching the house, from a distance, I saw my mother sitting by the culvert outside the house. I saw her wiping away her tears and I expected trouble.

And true enough, when I came close to her, she cried out, "We have been trying to get you on your car phone..."

"What has happened?" I asked.

Sensing my mother's distress, the driver helped her to walk back to the house, and as she was walking she told me that my brother had a stroke, and was lying in bed.

When I went into his room, I saw my brother lying on the bed. The right side of his body had been affected. He looked at me sadly as he held out his left hand to me. I squeezed his hand and said, "Don't worry, we shall get you walking in no time." I tried to reassure him. His oldest son, Peter, was by his side, and he also tried to reassure his father, "Don't worry dad, we will pull through this episode together."

"Don't let Dicky know about my health, it will disturb his concentration in his studies..." Kian Seng warned us, about his second son who was in his final year, studying in the USA.

IF YOU HAVE

SOMETHING TO DO

DO IT PROPERLY

IF YOU HAVE

SOMETHING TO SAY

SAY IT NICELY

Kian Seng's wife was too distressed to do anything, she kept to herself in a corner, weeping. We made the necessary arrangements to have him registered in a private hospital, and weeks later, Kian Seng was able to smile a little, but couldn't get up from the bed on his own.

After his discharge from the private hospital, Kian Seng moved into our home in Kuala Lumpur. His hospital bill was another challenge for the family, because he didn't have a life insurance policy. However, coping with those challenges one at a time, Peter sorted them out eventually.

A physiotherapist was called in to help him recover. Kian Seng had to learn to do things on his own, and his weak muscles had be quickly toned, or they would become useless. The exercises were strenuous, sometimes causing great pain. There were times when we wanted to tell the physiotherapist to go easy on him when we saw the pain on his face.

But we knew if we did that, Kian Seng would never recover enough to be able to do things on his own again. He had to go through pain and learn to adjust to the new conditions. Financially, he was down and out. Kian Seng was a very lonely and sick man. His self-esteem had been badly damaged. The only thing that kept him going was the hope that he would get up and walk like a normal man again. My wife and I stayed by his side, nursing him daily. Financially, we helped out whenever, and wherever we felt it was appropriate.

A year went by. He had made some progress and was able to move about on his own, but in an uncomfortable way.

"The $800 we invested in the boy (me) has finally paid off, Kian Seng," my mother said to Kian Seng. Hearing this, tears began to well-up in his eyes. Kian Seng was moved by these reminders. Traditionally, Asians think that males are assets to the family, and females are the opposite. However, in modern times, things have changed. I empathised with

WHEN YOU GET INTO

AN

UNCONTROLLABLE SITUATION

LEARN TO ADJUST

DON'T LEARN TO BLAME,

DON'T CURSE,

AND DON'T GIVE UP

JUST LEARN TO ADJUST

Kian Seng, but I never sympathised him, and that's the secret of coping with family pressures. To empathise is to understand with logic, not getting yourself emotionally involved in the dilemma. Had I sympathised with him, and get emotionally involved in the dilemma, I wouldn't have been of any use. Tears do not help in any situation. Advices, encouragement and financial support was needed at that time. And I went all the way!

Kian Seng had to live through another blow. It was the last day of 1988. I was booked to appear the year-end party in a ballroom filled with some 1500 distributors. I had been at the hotel since 3.00 pm that afternoon. The organiser had provided a room for my convenience. The night was filled with excitement over the event combined with lots of gifts and souvenirs given away by the organiser.

The grand finale was to usher in the new year. There was hugging and screams, laughter and cries, handshakes and kisses… Shortly after that, I excused myself and bid good-bye to the organiser with a handshake, as he gently tucked an envelope into the palm of my hand. I slowly slipped it into my coat pocket.

When You Know
You Have Done Well
You Sleep Better

I walked out from the hotel lobby, told the bell-captain to page for my driver, and shortly after that he was in the foyer of the hotel. "Let's go home." I told my driver. In the car, I switched on the reading light and reached into my pocket for the envelope. I opened it and as I had expected, it was my paycheck - RM2000. Not bad. I took a deep breath, satisfied, but really exhausted. I switched off the reading light… dozed off.

When I got home, I found a note on my bedroom door. Someone had scribbled on it in a hurry, "go back to Port Dickson ASAP, something has happened!"

The first thought that came to my mind was, "Could it be my brother...or my mother?" I dared not think further. To confirm my curiosity, I called Port Dickson.

My sister-in-law answered. I asked her what had happened "It's Dicky, in the USA. This afternoon we received a call from his friend in St. Louis that he had died in a car accident." I could hardly believe what I was hearing.

"Has Kian Seng been told of the bad news?" I asked.

"No, we have been waiting for you to break the news to him." She was afraid the news could cause my brother to have a heart attack.

"What about my mother?" I asked.

"She doesn't know either, but she is away in Port Klang, visiting a friend. She will be staying there the next few days," she quivered.

Telling to my mother would be another challenge. When I arrived at Port Klang, it was approximately 3.30 in the morning. When the news was broken to my mother, she walked out to the garden, looked up at the night sky and screamed her head off. "God, why would you take the innocent? Here! Take me instead, I'm ready to trade with you. You have been so unfair! First, you didn't want to spare my son, and now you take my grandson." She beat her chest as she cursed at the night sky.

To avoid lights popping up in the entire neighbourhood, we literally lifted her into the car, and drove off. It was approximately a two hour drive from Port Klang to Port Dickson. My mother was still displaying her agitation by talking to the gods as though there were negotiations going on. "Look, I need to think of how I am going to break the news to Kian Seng, please would you be silent and let me concentrate?" I begged her.

She seemed to have rationalised what I had said, and the rest of the journey was quiet.

The night sky seemed dark with hopelessness, I felt sad, but it was beyond anyone's control. When we arrived at the house, there was more weeping and searching for an explanation. When Kian Seng woke up, it was about 8.00 am. I saw him limping uneasily down the stairs, smiling and asking, "What brought you here so early?" he asked.

I reached out to support him on the stairway, helped him to the dining table where a simple breakfast consisting of a slice of bread and a cup of chocolate drink was laid out.

The hardest part was breaking the news to him. I sat him down, smiled and asked him how he was. As we were exchanging small talk, I was trying to think of the best way to break the news to him, to ensure that his delicate heart could withstand the bad news.

After going through all possible things to say, I found there was no gentle way to break the news, so I took a deep breath and said, "Listen, I have something I need to urgently tell you." Kian Seng looked at me, wondering what could possibly go wrong at this hour, when everyone was at home. "What?"

"I need you to be strong, and not to cause any more damage than there already is," I wanted to be sure.

"OK," he assured.

"Dicky met with an automobile accident in the USA. And he is not going to come back to us any more!" I finally broke the news, and I must admit that I had expected him to collapse right there on the table.

"You mean…" he wasn't sure, but was curious.

"Yes, he died." My heart went out to Kian Seng.

THE TRUTH ABOUT LEAVING IS

EVERYONE HAS TO LEAVE

ONE WAY OR ANOTHER

THE QUESTION IS

WHO LEAVES FIRST?

There was a moment of silence, everyone was expecting the worst. You could hear a pin drop, then suddenly everyone started crying together, as though it was a well rehearsed show. Seeing my mother crying and my brother holding on to the only framed graduation photo of Dicky and talking to himself, and crying, I was unable to control the emotion I had kept within me for so many hours. I broke down finally.

We spent the first few days of 1989 in the rituals of Dicky's burial. Finally, he was laid to rest. The whole episode was so melancholic. My brother had to keep on with his struggle. Peter, his eldest son would take the leading role in keeping the family going from then on. The truth about parting with loved ones is harsh; the fact is everyone has to die some day, the question is who will die first? The one who dies later has to shed more tears, and bear more pain than those who leave earlier.

My schedule in 1989 was tight, I was travelling all over the world as well as taking care of my local clients. One day, when I returned from abroad, the driver was waiting for me at the Subang International Airport. "Boss, Peter called. Asked you to call back," my driver told me.

I got the news that my brother had just passed away. I told the driver to take me to Port Dickson right away. When I got home where we had just recently gone through the ceremony of another death, I saw my brother lying in the middle of the hall. I went near his body, and I saw my mother, sitting alone by the windows. Her face had turned pale, and she had aged greatly. I studied her for a moment.

Then, I went over to my brother's body lying there motionless. As if wanting to talk to him, I saw his tie wasn't properly tied, so I tried to adjust it. I couldn't do it properly because my eyes were full of tears and I could barely see.

Then, a tear dropped down onto my brother's shirt, I wiped it and suddenly, I found myself hugging him, "please don't go, not now. Please don't go. I don't hate you any more, what you did and said to me when I was younger, all that has been forgotten and forgiven, please don't go..." I begged him. I felt a hand pulling me away from my brother's body and a voice saying, "Let him go, David. Let him go." It was my brother's good friend who was there to pay his last respect. He consoled me.

WE ARE PERCEIVED DIFFERENTLY

BY OTHERS

IF YOU HAD BEEN

PERCEIVED AS BAD,

THEN DO GOOD

IN ORDER TO CORRECT

THE PERCEPTION

I don't blame my brother and others who had different perceptions about me.

They must have got some pretty good reasons. Similarly, no one gets annoyed with somebody for nothing, there must be a valid reason. I was mischievous when I was a young boy, I must have been a great disappointment to them. That's how we can be perceived. Perceptions can be permanent if not repaired or attended to. Here was a classic opportunity for me to repair the poor perception my brother had of me.

Remember, when we are young, we are perceived differently. The more fortunate kids are loved, and cared for every minute of their lives. They are surrounded by people who are attentive to their needs and wants, and they grew up to become people with strong self esteem. While the less fortunate ones are treated quite differently. Many are abused both verbally and physically. The less fortunate ones may grow up with the stigma of being a 'rejected specimen.' They may be imbued with malicious thoughts and meanness.

However, regardless of the background you may have had, when it is time to cope with family challenges, remember, this may be the only time in your life to prove your worth. You may be now judged well by the people who had once had misunderstood you.

Now, you may say, why should I live up to someone else's expectation? Or, why should I bother about people who once mistreated me?

Well, to answer both these questions, yes, you can go on living in an isolated world of your very own, where no one is good enough for you, but where does it get you?

Try to level with me. Wouldn't it be better to win back some of the people who had misjudged you once and continue with a life long, healthy relationship. Life is not for getting back at someone, neither is it for getting even. It is for laughing, loving and living.

Always provide the best support in whatever ways you can, rather than have an attitude of couldn't-care-less just because you were illiterate earlier, if you get even one chance, show that you are who you really are – someone with a heart.

In the same year, 1989, through a series of networks, I came in contact with another very interesting man, Robert Hubbard, who became a good friend. Robert is a master salesman who came to Malaysia and started a network marketing company. From scratch, he managed to build the company into having a monthly sales turnover of RM40 million. Robert is a very hard working and capable distributor with great experience in this industry. He engaged me to speak for his herbal based company. We got along well, and enjoyed our friendship. Then, one day, Robert left for Canada, and I have not seen him since then. Apparently, the company he was managing had got into deep financial trouble, his partners had 'cleaned' him out totally. " David, you understand the politics I was getting in to, if I don't get out, I will be stranded in Malaysia forever. However, I shall get in touch with you as soon as I have something going," Robert called to tell me, from Toronto, Canada.

Well, I must say, the 80s were a decade of growth and progress. The good Lord watched over me and guided me at every step of the way. The income was good, some of the people I met along the way turned out to be special. Although there was some turbulence also. We must cope with such situations without creating more tension which might affect our lives badly. All said and done the entire decade was fabulous.

EVERY ONCE IN A WHILE

THERE WILL COME

A TURBULENCE

WHICH MAY ROCK YOU...

EITHER TO BE

STRONGER OR WEAKER

5

Another Chapter in the Profession

The Hyatt Hotel in Hong Kong is perhaps one of the most beautiful hotels I have stayed in. The hospitality they offered left a good impression that has lasted till today. Judy and I arrived there for a sales convention. It was the third month of 1990. The Chinese lunar year had just finished. The weather in Hong Kong was still cold then. We were in the hotel room, and I said to Judy, "I really don't know what's in store for us in this decade. But I have a good feeling that it will definitely be better than the last."

"How do you know?" she asked.

"Because I want it to be!" I was confident.

"Well, in that case, I am looking forward to it then..." she concluded.

Judy and I spent another three days relaxing at the hotel instead of packing up and leaving on the scheduled date. The three days did me good. I had an opportunity to work on my new training materials.

On the second day, the phone rang at 3.30 in the morning. "Who would call me at this hour I wondered," I was surprised to hear Jim's voice. " David, please call Robert Hubbard in Sydney as soon as you get back to Kuala Lumpur." He sounded urgent. As soon as I got back, I called Robert.

"Hi Robert, how are you and what are you doing in Sydney?" I asked enthusiastically. Robert told me that he had just started a network marketing company in Australia, and would like some training to be done.

"The last one year, I have been working hard putting this outfit together, and now we have approximately 6,000 distributors all across Australia. Fly in tomorrow if you can," he suggested.

I left the next evening, and the flight to Sydney took about eight hours. I was fresh in the morning and flying business class is always very refreshing. By the time I got out of the terminal, Robert came to meet me.

We hugged each other, and felt good meeting up once again. I spent the next week with Robert, going through the details of the programmes. On several occasions, Jim joined us for dinner. "There is a substantial amount of work to be done in the company, you may want to concentrate more here. Forget about Malaysia for a while, there is plenty for you to do here." Robert told me.

Being my partner, Jim naturally didn't welcome the idea of my concentrating on Australia alone. "David, I like Robert's idea, however, we have obligations to our many clients overseas, we can't just dump them and concentrate here," he told me one evening over dinner. "Jim, rest assured. I will not do anything to jeopardise our business". Over the next few days we discussed how to balance all the training services that I needed to address, and the conclusion was that I would spend more time in Australia than in Malaysia. "Even for a single programme in Malaysia, you need to fly back to address it. You must travel from Sydney to Malaysia as though you are travelling from your home to the city of Kuala Lumpur." Jim wanted to be reassured, and I gave him that assurance.

There was still plenty of work to do done in Malaysia as well as in Robert's company. I would sometimes work with Robert for two months in Sydney, and then return to Kuala Lumpur to attend to some clients' need. Judy would travel with me from time to time, as she was expecting our first child. The workload was not too strenuous, I was careful not to cross that line. Robert was also very considerate.

My Old Ambition Relived

One day, an old friend, Gary Chong, came on a visit and stayed with us in our Sydney home for a week. To ensure my hospitality was well rendered, I took him to many wonderful places in New South Wales. As usual, we preferred the idea of a barbeque rather than cooking a meal for the family and Gary. While we were setting up the barbeque, Gary advised me that I should return to Kuala Lumpur more often. I told Gary that I had enough to do here.

"Listen, there are a few people from a publishing company that I personally know, who might be interested in publishing your work," Gary said.

"What do you mean publishing my work?" I asked enthusiastically.

"Getting your experience transformed into a book." Gary continued.

"You mean they might be keen to publish my work?" I reconfirmed.

"Yes, that's what I mean," Gary reaffirmed.

The next day, Jim came by and I asked for his advice. "David, this is what you have been waiting for all your life, go for it!" Jim was confident.

In the next few days, I finished my work and headed for Kuala Lumpur. "Let's upgrade your ticket to business class," I told Gary. The next day we flew back to Kuala Lumpur.

The meeting with my publishers, *Times Publishing*, was pleasant. We decided to write two books within a year. When I came out of their office, I felt exhilarated. With little experience of writing, I set out to write my first book: *The Making of A Super Salesperson*. It took me some six months;

travelling between Kuala Lumpur and Sydney, writing and attending to training classes was extremely satisfying too.

When the book was complete. I thought it would be worthwhile getting a speaker friend from the USA to launch it for me. I went through my list. Bob Pecor, America's sales wizard was the best choice.

After some hard negotiations, Bob and his wife flew in from the USA.

"Don't worry, all expenses shall be taken care of by me, personally," I assured Bob.

For the launch of the book, my local promoter, Latifi Nordin & Company, had managed to sell out the functions in Kuala Lumpur, Penang as well as in East Malaysia. More than 4,000 copies of the book sold at the launching. Some 10,000 copies were sold within the first year of publication. That gave me much confidence, and I felt really good about it. Then, my second book was also published. The press was very helpful, they had supported me in many ways, giving me the spotlight whenever I needed it. I began to write more and soon the third book came rolling out from the publisher's office, then the fourth , fifth and so on... An old ambition was being realised.

To become an author had been my lifelong ambition. As you may recall, many publishers in the past didn't want to represent me, but I never gave up that dream...that ambition. I kept it aside, not knowing when it would come true, and finally when it did, I did what I had to do. I put in the best I could!

Likewise, it is the same in your case. The ambition that you once had, may seem far away. It almost disappeared from your mind. You may have given up and gone on to something else. However, let me remind you, when it reappears before you, don't let it go, give it your best shot, make the best of it!

SOME DREAMS ARE OLD

THE OLDER THEY GET...

SOMETIMES,

THE BETTER

THEY WILL BE

Plato's ring of influence was at work. Ever since I started writing professionally, I have also managed to motivate many others to write as well. And I am glad that this ring of influence is working out well – that's what I mean by motivation. We motivate others, so that they can motivate some more. As you may recall, there weren't many authors in Malaysia in the early days. When I first got into writing in the 80s, though I had to publish my work myself it was an example to many others that they could too.

"If David can do it, anyone can!" I used to say that in my seminar. As my good friend and platform associate, Jeffrey Chew, who also is the author of *From Zero to Hero*, very nicely put it over lunch at the Regent Hotel in the City a number of years ago, " David, you may not have noticed it, but in Malaysia you were the one who gave most of us the motivation and the self-esteem to be a writer. We took a look at your book and we asked ourselves if David, a Form Three dropout can do it, we certainly can do it as well."

Plato had said, *"This gift which you have…is not an art, but an inspiration: there is a divinity moving you, like that in the stone which Euripides calls a magnet, but which is commonly known as the stone of Heracles. For that stone not only attracts iron rings, but also imparts to them a similar power of attracting other rings; and sometimes you may see a number of pieces of iron and rings suspended from one another so as to form a long chain; and all of them derive their power of suspension from the original stone. Now this is like the Muse, who first gives men inspiration herself and from these inspired persons a chain of other persons is suspended, who take the inspiration from them."*

Bob Pecor, America's sales wizard said to me during our flight home from East Malaysia, " David, your good lifestyle is admired by many. Your friends who had come to your house, couldn't help but feel that one day they would like to have what you have. A lovely home, luxury cars, a good lifestyle, a loving and healthy family, and most of all, your capabilities. You have given them a vision and a direction. They will now work hard and hope to retire early with the kind of lifestyle you are enjoying these days. I think that's the greatest motivation one can give others."

Are You The One Who Motivates Or Are You The One Who Debilitates Others

That's the true essence of how I would term motivation. Motivation does not mean being fearful or jealous of what others might learn from you. Motivation does not mean others shouldn't have what you have. It is about sharing, giving and encouraging. Your job is to hand down that ring of influence, so others can pass it on. I am glad I have done just that. And one day, when I lay down to rest, I will know I have done what was needed as a human being…not only as a motivator, that I have been called all my life.

Subsequently, I sent one of my bestsellers to Og Mandino, shortly before his death, and I said to him, "Thank you for all you have done. This is the product of your legacy, Og." I spoke with pride, and he felt great.

Subsequently, he sent a copy of his *Trilogy of the Greatest*, and he wrote, "Keep up the good work. Remember, what you have done is putting your thoughts on paper, compiled and printed into what we call a book. People buy and read what you have written. Keep striving to bestow good wisdom, what better way can one lead a life as an author of good advice?" Og's words meant so much to me.

The Bestseller Dream

Singapore, early December,1995. I came back to the hotel suite after a long hard day in the Sun City convention centre. It was almost 7.00 in the evening, the receptionist was courteous and ever-smiling, " Good evening, Mr. Goh," she greeted.

"Hi, how have you been today?" I asked, reciprocating with a good gesture.

"Very well. I have been meeting some very nice people today," she said.

"That's nice." I left the reception after she handed me the key to my suite.

When I got into my suite, I noticed there was a fax on the table, and next to it was a basket of fruits, with a note of greeting from the hotel manager. I looked through the basket, took out a banana, and sat down to go through the fax.

The fax was from Taipei, Taiwan. It was from a man named David Chu. He wrote, " Mr. Goh, I didn't get the chance to attend your seminar in Singapore, I had to rush back due to some urgency. However, I am a publisher in Taiwan and I would like to represent you as your promoter. Call me at this number whenever you have the time." I glanced at my wrist watch, it showed 7.35 pm.

Should I call him now? I wondered. Then I thought, why not. And I called.

In the next few days, Judy and I arrived in Taipei from Sydney. "The weather is pretty cold today," said the driver who had come to pick us up. The Grand Hyatt in Taipei had arranged for our airport transfer in style, in a limousine, when we arrived in the evening at the CKS International Airport. December is usually a rather warm month in Sydney, but fortunately, we had been warned to take along some warm clothing.

The ride took us about 40 minutes or so to the Grand Hyatt in the city of Taipei. When we checked in, there was a note from David Chu at the counter. "Welcome to Taipei.

Please have the receptionist call me when you arrive. We shall have dinner together."

I handed the number to the receptionist, and the call was put through.

During dinner, we discussed the possibility of conducting seminars in Taipei with an interpreter.

The next day, David Chu came to the hotel. We had breakfast and then he drove us to his office. I presented him my set of books, we discussed further, and he said to me, "Let us begin with this book, *52 Ways To Make More Money In Network Marketing,*" indicating his desire to get that book translated and hold the first seminar on the same subject.

Half a year went by. I was still very much in contact with David Chu, and besides those seminars I had to look after Robert Hubbard and the rest of my clients in Malaysia.

Handling the Situation And Keeping Your Cool

As scheduled, the seminar had been planned for June 29th, 1996. I had several engagements in Sydney in the month of June, and could manage to leave for Taipei only on June 28th morning by Qantas.

The flight took us to Brisbane for a stopover and to pick up more passengers. The stopover was supposed to be 45 minutes, however, an hour went by, and then the captain announced that they had some mechanical problem with the aircraft, so he asked us to be patient and wait a while. And we waited.

More waiting. Four hours went by. We were quickly ushered into a lounge by the ground crew of Qantas. By this time, some of the passengers had became unruly, and demanded full compensation. The flight operations director and high ranking officers of Qantas appeared, trying to deal with some of the irate passengers. The situation was getting really out of hand.

Free overseas phone calls were made available to everyone on that flight. I called David Chu and explained what was happening. We spoke about the possibility of arriving late and how to get over to Kaoshung for the first program.

Then I called Judy in Sydney and she was surprised to hear that I was still in Brisbane after so many hours.

I kept my cool, there was nothing I could do except pray.

I told the good Lord that if He had other plans for me, I would leave that to Him, otherwise, He must ensure that I get into Taipei by early 29th morning.

It was well over six hours then they finally fixed the mechanical problem. We were told to assemble for boarding, and then suddenly, we were again told to remain in the lounge.

"What the hell is going on here?" One of the passengers lost his cool and shouted. More joined in. The very high ranking officers were apologising to the passengers.

"May I have your attention, Ladies and Gentlemen," one of the officers spoke at last.

"There is a law in Australia that an airline pilot cannot fly a plane after exceeding certain hours at work.. And we have to abide by the law. " This caused more sparks.

More shouting.

"However, they have just dispatched another crew from Sydney, and it should be arriving very soon," the officer continued.

"Fly us into Taipei and refund us when we arrive there!" another passenger shouted. Sensing that there was an opportunity, more passengers joined in that unreasonable demand.

"Look, I can't make any decision on this issue. What we should do now is remain calm and wait for the new crew to come. The important thing is to get you into Taipei by today," said the officer.

"So, now you want to push your responsibility to the Qantas office in Taipei; settle the problem here, before you fly us out," warned one of the passengers.

"Listen, I will sue Qantas for this delay!" another one said.

"If you don't agree to the refund, we won't board the flight." More threats.

It was beyond anyone's control. The officers and ground crew could do nothing, they could only listen to the passengers' grievances.

A lady officer came over to me during the commotion she sat down next to me, she said, "Listen, I am sorry for what has happened. There is...really nothing anyone can do about it. And I appreciate you keeping your cool. By the way, what do you do for a living?"

"No, I am not a reporter, if that's what's bothering you. I am writing down the entire event for my own personal evaluation. And I think it is wrong to make unreasonable demands in a situation beyond control," I assured her.

"Thank you for being so understanding," she returned with a smile. I sat there witnessing the entire scenario. I had a hard time keeping up with their demands, trying my best to jot down every detail in my journal, and hoping one day it would be of some use.

That's why high ranking officers are paid such high salaries. They have to handle all kinds of situations, without causing more apprehension, I thought.

When the crew finally arrived, we had already had our dinner. We boarded the plane and flew out of Brisbane at about ten that evening.

I called David Chu and told him the expected time of arrival, and asked that he be at the airport to pick me up.

When we got into the plane, every passenger was bribed with a bottle of *Issey Miyake*, a branded perfume from Japan. As a business class passenger, I was also bribed with a bottle

ALWAYS,

THERE ARE TWO WAYS

TO HANDLE A SITUATION

KEEP YOUR COOL

OR BLOW YOUR TOP

CHOOSE THE ONE

THAT PREVENTS

FURTHER DAMAGE

of expensive wine and a bottle of Champagne. That shut up everyone…I supposed.

By the time I woke up, it was almost daybreak. I glanced at my watch, it was 5.00 am. Breakfast was prepared and by the time we landed at CKS International, it was 6.35 am.

David Chu hurriedly drove us to another airport to take a flight to Koashung. I was exhausted, tired but excited. Finally when we arrived at the packed convention centre, my enthusiasm overcame my exhaustion, I no longer felt tired. I didn't fail David Chu, as I had promised him.

My relationship with David Chu deepened as the years went by. Through 1996-1999, David Chu never failed to surprise me with his capability to organise a mass rally, attended by thousands of people from all over Taiwan.

David Chu successfully marketed a million copies of my book *52 Ways To Make More Money In Network Marketing* to the People's Republic of China. With that, my book became a bestseller in a very short span of time.

Today, we call him Dr David Chu, for he has worked hard to enrich himself academically. He was conferred a Ph.D by Professor Dr Derick Bricham from Phoenix International University. Dr David Chu now represents Phoenix International University in Taiwan, China and Hong Kong. Occasionally, we still bump into each other in different parts of the world. David Chu, an incredible character, with a very strong integrity, has been a constant source of energy and support to me.

The Right People,
The Right Timing,
You Will See The Right Result!

Robert Hubbard sold his network marketing company in Australia in 1994 for a handsome price, and left for Canada. And I had no desire to work with others. I had a discussion with Judy and suggested that we spend the next two to three years in Australia. " Look, since we have nothing much to do here, and the lifestyle is great, I can embark from here to service the clients overseas. Moreover, Jim will be glad to have me around more often," I told her.

We agreed. Then, we began a lifestyle of a more relaxed type. Taking things as they came. We began to travel around Australia, taking pictures and jotting down all details in my journal for my future books. Jim and I travelled to different parts of Australia and the nearby countries to see some of our clients. On weekends, I would take my family to the park, visit friends or just drive around in the city. More often than not, the family preferred to eat out rather than messing around in the kitchen. Jim and his girl friend would come by to have coffee daily. Besides all this, I was still very much in touch with my clients in different parts of the world—Taiwan, Canada, USA, as well as Malaysia. Meanwhile, Judy was pregnant. She chose to stay home instead of travelling around with me so often. Time went by.

June 8th 1996, Delena came to join the family. She was born in the middle of winter. "And here is the kangaroo that you have been carrying around for several months all over Australia!" declared the doctor.

"Wrong, besides Australia, this kangaroo had been to China, Taiwan, Hong Kong and the USA," I interrupted.

Like all proud parents, we looked at Delena with pride and love, I said to her, "Welcome to the family. You are going to be loved, cared for and enjoy a meaningful life with us."

A few months went by. The weather began to warm up. One day, when the kids and I were in the pool, Judy suggested that we barbeque at the poolside instead of going out to eat. While the kids and I were in the pool, I saw Judy setting up the barbeque. She moved swiftly in and out of the house so often. "Too much work," I said to myself.

Then I began thinking about the good times we had in Malaysia. And the convenience of having a maid to do our daily chores and a chauffeur to drive us around. I began to think about the good points of Malaysia. Whereas, in Australia, literally everything from clearing the garbage to mowing the lawn, scrubbing the kitchen to cleaning the toilet, from looking out and waiting for a place to park the car to shampooing the car, everything had to be done by ourselves.

"Let's go back," I rationalised with Judy, and the kids. I explained to her that we could return any time we felt like it, moreover, there was still the piece of land we owned—and we could have a contractor build a home for us, of our own design. "Beside, we can get to eat the food we have missed, the laksa, fried kuey-teow, mee-rubus, and your favorite rojak!" I encouraged Judy. And that was it.

6

Touching Others

Our lives are, to an extent, shaped and touched by others. We are what we are today because of someone's touch. Their kind words, and their encouragement make and shape the person we are. The 'Greats' in the industry, became great because someone said something to them that changed their outlook and entire concept of living. On the other hand, there are also countless individuals who were driven to despondency, and misery, living in the most unfortunate way. These unfortunate ones also were shaped like you and me in the early stages of their lives by others. That's why it is important that you send out positive touches to others.

We must ask ourselves everyday if we have touched someone? Your kind words, and encouraging remarks will eventually return to you ten fold. Do you remember who was the one who shaped you? Who was your mentor in the beginning?

Everyone has a mentor. Some have more than one, while some others have a mentor in every phase of their lives. It is vital that you don't forget your mentor. I remember Ronnie Yu, who gave me so much encouragement in my early days as a labourer, then it was Mohammad Isa, one of the most remarkable motivators in the early 70s. When I got into this arena as a speaker, Zig Ziglar became my mentor. When I got into writing, the late Og Mandino became another mentor of mine. These are the mentors in my life. And I will always cherish the moments I spent with them, their kind words, and encouraging remarks. They touched and shaped me to become what I am today. Like the cycle of life, I went on to touch others, both from the platform and in one-on-one coaching.

These are just some of the people whose lives were touched by others, inspired by others and now they are touching others, inspiring others. Like a wheel within a wheel, it whirls round and round. This is what I mean by positive touches. There are well over thousands of people, CEOs, marketing gurus, and professionals who are shaping others and touching others, either by platform selling or just by saying comforting and encouraging words. Have you encouraged someone today? If you have, then you are shaping others just like these people. Did you speak comforting words to someone this week? If you did, then I welcome you into the world of mentoring. You don't have to be a celebrity or a motivator or a great speaker in order to touch someone. You can begin by saying the right thing at the right time.

What we are today is because someone took the trouble to help, touch and shape us. And if you appreciate that, why not touch or shape someone from now on?

Paul Low, CEO of BHLB
Pacific Trust

Mohan Das - The Malaysian
who scaled Mt Everest

Dr Mahathir Mohammad -
The Prime Minister

Datuk Azahar - The sailor
who went solo around the
world

Gan Ah Seng - A powerful
motivator and Dr Andrew
Goh, an excellent trainer
from Singapore

Krissana Kritmanorote -
The Thai Life Insurance Agent
who went on to inspire mi llions

The late Princess Diana

Zig Ziglar - author of
'See You at the Top'

Charles 'Tremendous'
Jones, Author of "Life is
Tremendous"

Joe Girard - The greatest
salesman in the world

Diana Golden -
The one legged skier

Nido Qubein - author and
speaker

Dr Martin Luther King Jr.

Robert Pecor - Sales wizard

My late mother

Cavett Robert

Mike Podolinsky and wife,
Sarnai

Charlie Chan,
CEO of SK Brothers

Mother Theresa

Bruce Lee - A legend

Donald Trump

Antony Robbins -
A great motivator of the
modern day

Mohammad Ali

Dato' Michelle Yeoh
Pride of the Nation

Poh Teck Lim -
Author and Speaker

Billy Lim -
Author and Speaker

Max Muniz of New York Life
and my wife Judy

Mark

Tan Onn Poh and Phang Wai Yeen - Marketing Gurus

Robert Hubbard,
Business from Canada

Amos Yap,
Vice President - Training
ING Insurance Bhd

Dr David Chu, Taiwan

Abdul Harith Abdullah,
CEO-ACM

Dr Norman Vincent Peale

Billy Graham

AK Wong, CEO of OAC Bhd

Tom Kho -
A great life insurance agent

Art Linkletter – Celebrity

Jerry Yang, Founder, Yahoo

Jackie Chan

Prof. David Chu and friends from
Taiwan

Bobby Curtola -
Canada's Rock & Roll
Legend

Andrew Carnegie

Mary Kay Ash,
Founder, Mary Kay
Cosmetics

Lily, Dottie and Bob Walters

Dato' Lawrence Chan Kum Peng

Ray Spies – Speaker

Peter Yu, New York Life

Rev. Dr Philip Tan, Senior Pastor, Christ Lutheran Church

Rax Maughan, CEO Forever Living Products, USA

Pastor Ong, Assistant Pastor Christ Lutheran Church

Ong Pin Hean, Allianz Life

Tunku Abdul Rahman -
The first prime minister of Malaysia

Auri Watanan,
World Rally driver

Rich Devos,
Founder - Amway

Og Mandino, Author:
Greatest Series

Tan Sri Saleh Sulong,
Chairman, DRB-
Hicom, Malaysia

Steven Tring, Businessman
and speaker

7

A Whole World
– A New Frontier

Let's Return To Malaysia

In December 1996, we packed up and left Australia. As promised, the desired bungalow for Judy was built by 1997, and we moved in. Judy got a maid to help her out in her daily chores, and I got a chauffeur for my own convenience. We still travel to many parts of the world every year, either for my scheduled engagements or for holidays. The kids are back in school and the youngest, Delena, clings to us all day long.

My family

The year 1998 was another busy one for engagements. Clients in Malaysia got to know that I was back in town, and bookings naturally increased because now they did not have to incur expenses like my airfares from Sydney, Australia.

I was back selling my books from the platform, and that year alone I managed to push more than 12,000 copies of *Step Into The Future With Nothing* in its 6th edition.

My mother's health was failing, she was getting weaker. She was 96 years old. She was getting a little difficult to handle, and we decided that she must be nursed professionally. So we put her in a 'home care' where she was looked after by a nurse. Despite my busy schedule, I would often drive my mother to our house to have dinner or lunch with us. When she was 97, she had to move about in a wheelchair, for her fragile body was getting weaker and smaller daily, and gradually she was too weak to even hold a spoon herself. One day, while I was feeding her at the dining table, in her weak, soft voice, she said to me, "Son, you know when you were hardly one year old, you were a difficult child, you cried every night, and my sister and I just didn't know what to do then. You were driving us crazy, so we decided to send you to a nanny in another place to look after you, and it was two years later that you came back and stayed with us. I don't blame you for sending me to the nursing home, and I know it can be difficult for you to take care of me, especially when you are so busy with your schedule. I am proud of you and am glad that you are my son." I gently passed the spoon to Judy and told her to continue feeding my mother because tears were flooding my eyes. I couldn't hold up my emotions any longer, and left to go to the washroom. That was probably the last sensible thing my mother said to me during the last two years of her life. She died shortly after that.

In the same year, I met up with Mr S.K. Ghai, who became a friend and my publisher, and since then Sterling International has been very supportive in whatever I do.

Mr Ghai ensures that I am given all support. Four books have been published since then. These books are: *52 Ways To Make More Money In Network Marketing, Effective Sponsoring Skills, Making A Career* and my latest with him *From Zero to Millions – The LKH Story.* Three of the four books focus on the area of network marketing.

A very hard working man, Mr Ghai makes frequent trips to Malaysia and each time we meet, our friendship gets stronger. "Friends are like needle and thread You cannot sew with only one," I tell my friend, Mr Ghai.

Friends Are Like
Needle and Thread
Can't Do Much
Without One Another

In December 1998, Judy and I visited our old friend, Robert Hubbard in Vancouver. " I am giving a year-end party. There will be many local celebrities and personalities present. Come and join us. Pick up your ticket in the MAS office, I have arranged two business class tickets for you and Judy," Robert had told me earlier in our telephone conversation.

It was our first trip to Vancouver. I had been to Montreal few years ago, where I met Bobby Curtola, who is Canada's rock 'n roll legend. This time in Vancouver, I met Bobby again. We spent some time together. Judy and I were invited to a 'jamming' session with Bobby and his band players.

"I would like you to meet a gentleman who will be able to help you build up your career to another plateau," Robert told me at his year-end party with some business people and friends in the downtown Hotel Vancouver. We proceeded to another table where three couples were seated. All of them were properly attired, the men in tuxedos and the ladies elegantly dressed.

"Peter, I would like you to meet David." One of the gentlemen stood up, and extended his hand to me, and I did what I was supposed to do.

We sat down with the others, and Robert proceeded with more introductions of me. After a few minutes of exchanging ideas and business propositions, I told Peter: "I will have my set of books sent to your office tomorrow morning."

Peter Harris, in his early 50s has a very strong network with business people in North America. In a very short time, Peter was able to organise a group of business people for an evaluation to our AMMODAGO – The Art of Motivational Skill—5 day workshop that was scheduled in 1999. With that introduction, I returned to Vancouver a number of times subsequently that year. I am grateful to Robert for the numerous business introductions he has given since I came to know him. He is an unusual guy, witty and fits in well at every occasion.

In the same year, 1999, Robert and Bobby Curtola came to visit us at our home in Kajang. We invited them to stay with us for over a month, during which we had the opportunity for a cultural exchange while we enhanced our friendship. I

Students of AMMODAGO

had managed to postpone some speaking engagements to make time for writing. I completed two manuscripts by the end of the year, as scheduled.

The Millenium – Year 2000

Judy and I went to Shanghai. I was invited as a headline speaker for a company. I spoke for several hours, and then spent five days shopping and relaxing. One afternoon, Judy and her friends were out at a shopping centre.

I was in my suite jotting down the finer points in my journal. When that was done, I went to the dressing table to pick up something, and suddenly, I looked up to gaze at myself. I took some time to examine myself. A time for reflection... contemplation...or simply a time for a short self-examination. At the age of 47, my hair was almost white, wrinkles could be seen on my once youthful face. Poor eyesight was causing me great inconvenience. The dark circles around my eyes told me that I had overstrained them. I smiled and nodded in agreement. There was a sense of accomplishment and satisfaction within me.

Now, at the age of 50, I look back at the 26 years that have gone by since I began speaking professionally. And as an author, I have been writing for the past 20 years, and have successfully written more than 10 books which are sold in many countries. I will continue to write books because writing is my passion and my goal is to complete at least 25 books before my days are done on earth. My speaking engagements have been reduced tremendously these days. I accept only four engagements per month now. I also keep up with my personal development, playing golf with my buddies, swimming with my family and also taking guitar lessons. It is a new frontier for me. A world that is wholly new to me.

Naturally, those who once thought I couldn't do it have been proven wrong, and those who once thought I will never

be able to accomplish anything worthwhile have also been proven wrong! They are also a part of the people who have helped shape my life.

I hold no grudges against those who looked down on me once. As a matter of fact I am thankful that they persisted in thinking that I couldn't make it...I believe I was more determined because of them. I feel that the rules (society) should not dictate that those without proper paper qualifications should have less chance of success than those who have them. If one is willing to strive for it, if one is willing to go after one's dream, and willing to pay the price for success, the reward shouldn't be less for them than for those who rely on paper qualifications.

Right from the time I became a salesman, I had named the price of my own success, and there was only one way to get it done...through the people I knew.

Paper qualifications were just a stepping stone —a sort of yardstick to measure where you ought to begin when you get out from university. However, I must add that the paper qualifications are pieces of paper if one does not educate oneself further. I once heard someone say, "True education begins when your tertiary education ends." How true that is! One should never stop educating oneself after one graduates from college or university.

True Education Begins When Tertiary Education Ends.

The People Who Helped Shape Our Lives

The people who had helped shape our lives, where are they now? They are your networks. Part of true education comes from the network. It simply means that when you get into the society to work, you need friends to help you in achieving greater success. Think about it for a while. Isn't it true that we become financially successful because of the people we know, because they helped us in attaining success? The cars you own, the houses you have built and owned over the years, nothing came entirely on its own —it came from the support of your network. Of course, ultimately, we would like to think we accomplished it all by ourselves. Frank Sinatra once sang, "I did it my way..." but in reality, it is people, our network that does the job for us.

There is an ancient Chinese saying, "When you are at home, you depend upon your parents, when you are out there, you depend upon friends." The whole thing is a cycle. It goes round and round. Someone helped shape your life, you eventually will do the same for others. Yes, we become part of the shaping of a nation. Someone shaped us, and we shape others. No one is alone, unless he or she decides to be just that! Success, in whatever terms you may like to measure it, comes from the people we know, they contribute their share in shaping us.

My life wouldn't have changed so much if it hadn't been for the network that I developed in a short span of time.

Choosing the right people to mix with, who will help to shape us, is another faculty. When you mix with the wrong group, what is your chance for success? If you recall the very first part of my life, the people I mixed with when I was working as a labourer in Port Dickson were loafers who couldn't help themselves a bit, let alone help shape others. They kept themselves from success, from the attainment of further happiness and improvement.

They seek short-cuts in achieving successes, but these turn out to be the longer cuts! However, I must also warn you that it is very natural for us to be blinded by the people we mix with daily. We can't see their faults, we can see no wrong in these people. Just how can we know if they are right for us to mix with?

Identify Your Friends

Here are 10 characteristics that will give you further insight into the people you mix with. If they are negative, then I suggest that you move on to another group that is more dynamic, progressive and helpful for you. If you continue going around with such negative people, I am afraid you are going to end up acting like them and your chances of financial success and happiness will be minimal. If you look at people who are rich and who are happy and living in peace and harmony, I bet they have an attitude and characteristics that are totally the opposite of the negative people. Now, let's go through the list.

Negative – They see the dark side of everything.

Picky – They pick on every little issue, making a mountain out of a molehill. They calculate and they are unimpressive.

Gossip – Talking about other people is their pastime. They criticise other people's shortcomings and consideration for others is unheard of.

Unfair – Everything to them is unfair, from the education system to the economics of the country. From the weather to their neighbourhood. They complain about just everything under the sun. If others are doing well and better than them, they believe it is due to luck.

Hostile and Vengeful – They believe in getting even. They live in a malicious and hostile world. They can't rationalise in any situation, neither can they find a reason for being kind. Some of these people believe that the only way to settle a dispute is by fists and kicks.

Jealous – Jealousy is their trademark. They are jealous of other people's success. They speak untruth about others, they gossip and they attack. But they are denied their own success.

Proud – They go about their lives with false pride. They get hurt easily by the words or actions of others. They can't seem to control themselves in any given situation.

Egoistic – The very reason for their living is probably to boast about their unseen accomplishments, which only emanate from their mind. Their ego gets in their way every time they get a chance to talk. They are self-centered, and others are unimportant to them.

Disrespectful of Authority (Law) – They are always trying to challenge authority. Going against authority means winning to these people. They disregard authority, which most of the time gets them into trouble with the law. That's how you come to read about them in the news headlines. These people are always on the losing end. You may have heard it before—no one is above the law.

Inconsiderate – Such people always want to do things their way, and it doesn't matter if the way is wrong. For such people, getting the thing done is the only thing that matters. These are people who would trample upon anyone who comes in their way. And if others won't give in to them, then hostility follows.

8

The Day the Eagle Took Off

Once there was an old farmer who went up a hill to hunt for 'food'. He couldn't find any on that day. However, he came home with an eagle's egg. He didn't know what to do with the egg, so he put it with the rest of the eggs in the chicken's coop. A few days later, with the rest of the chicks, the young eagle was hatched.

As they grew up together, the chicks looked at the young eagle with amazement. They asked him numerous questions, "Why do you look so different from all of us? And why is your beak so long? And your claws, they look so gigantic and vicious? Your wings, why are they so huge as if you can fly?" These questions puzzled the young eagle.

The young eagle searched for answers but found none.

A few months went by. The young eagle was growing in size. He became muscled, arrogant and alert, yet he still played around with the rest of the chickens. They would play hide and seek daily in the open field, and would wait for the old farmer to give them food. When night fell, he would lead the chickens to the coop to rest for the night.

The young eagle live the life of a chicken, he thought like one, felt like one, acted and behaved like one. He became part of them. The young eagle knew nothing about flying.

One day, as usual, they were out in the open field…playing. And high above, in the blue sky, soared a huge bird – the father eagle.

Circling a few times, the father eagle was careful not to strike at first sight, careful enough not to scare his victims. He studied the vicinity and then he narrowed in like a laser beam, spreading his wings as he cut through the thin air, mercilessly diving straight into his victims.

His gaze fixed on his victims, the father eagle came closer to his objective for the day. As he got closer, he noticed something was wrong.

"What in the world is the young eagle doing with his 'food'?" the father eagle thought to himself.

However, he put the question out of his mind and continued to charge forward, the chickens had begun to run for shelter. The young eagle didn't know what was happening, he looked up in confusion. Not knowing what was to become of him, he waited for the father eagle to come charging down.

The father eagle was charging. As he came closer, he touched the ground with open claws, sending the dust flying everywhere – a sign of disappointment and anger. Then he took off and vanished within the clouds.

The young eagle could only watch in amazement.

"What was that? Looked like me and could fly…" he wondered as he went to look for his 'brothers and sisters'. He found them hiding in the chicken coop, and they continued playing again.

Author's note:
Similarly, some people look at others who are successful and declare that success is only meant for others and not for themselves. They watch others in surprise.

A few days went by; again, they went out in the open field. The father eagle was on a nearby hill…watching every move. He just couldn't believe what he was looking at. He figured that if the young eagle behaved like he had earlier, he would not even be able to get his food ever. So, he decided to teach the young eagle a lesson. Again, he came charging, diving through the thin air and landed in the open field some distance away from the young eagle.

The young eagle watched in bewilderment. Then he stomped through the open field, making his way uneasily to the father eagle. As he came closer, the father eagle turned his head, twisted his body and took off like a strike of lightning.

"Wow! Look how it takes off..." the young eagle said to himself.

"How in the world can he do that?" he wondered. Bewildered, he tried to explain it to himself by saying, "Maybe, the big bird is born lucky." As he said that, he turned to look for his 'brothers and sisters' again.

Author's note:
Likewise, it is the same with our lives. Some people look at others who are successful and wonder how they have done it, rather than find out ways to do so. Yet, there are many who will affirm that those who are successful are just born lucky. They consider luck as the ultimate reason for success. Their thinking is so shallow and limited that they begin to rely on luck rather than labour. If you read it as an acronym L.U.C.K actually represents Labour Under Correct Knowledge. Evidently, luck has a very little to do with your success, you still need to labour for it.

Day after day, the father eagle watched their movements from a distance. He came to the conclusion that as long as the young eagle was there, he could not be objective. "The only way is to talk him out of it," he thought to himself.

Finally, the father eagle landed in the open field and with watchful eyes, he looked around. The young eagle saw the father eagle and ran after him. The air was still, and the atmosphere was calm, as the young eagle made his way to the father eagle. The two of them seemed to be 'chatting' with each other for a few moments, and after that, the father turned and took off into the blue sky once again.

Author's note:
Once in a while, there comes a person in your life, whose words touch your heart or the fibre of your being, who sets you thinking and going. Anyone who can come into your life and inspire you to go further would then be your inspirational teacher. And with all your energy, you should strive to make a difference.

The 'small chat' they had turned out to be a new horizon and opened new possibilities for the young eagle. Next day, the young eagle was running and trying to stretch his wings, flipping awkwardly. The farmer noticed something was 'brewing' in the young eagle, but he couldn't figure out what. However, now the young determined eaglet had a new objective in his life. The rest of his 'brothers and sisters' were puzzled as well, so they went to ask him.

"What did the big bird say to you the other day?" they asked.

"He told me I could actually fly like him," the young eagle was honest.

Day after day, the young eagle went out in the open field, practising his take-off stance. Relentlessly, he would push himself to the limit, regardless of the weather or the time of day or night. Yard after yard, he would punish his aching body in order to lift himself off from the ground he had stood on for so long. Through perseverance, and dogged determination, the young eagle was able to lift himself one foot off the ground after months of merciless ordeal.

Soon, he was seen flying over the roof of the chicken coop, then over the pole, and subsequently, he was able to cruise in the blue sky, like the father eagle.

Author's note:
If you want to develop muscles in your body, you need to pump iron on a daily basis. You need to go to a gym to work out daily. To be healthy and physically fit, you need to go through the relevant physical exercises. To be a good student, you need to develop the habit of studying at home for a few hours each day. To be a good and outstanding salesperson, you need to get out of the office and make sales calls daily. One day is not sufficient for the job, neither can it be done in the next few days or weeks. Sometimes it takes years, however, if you are really determined, you would get it done within months. The fact remains that we need to get into action if we want to accomplish anything in life.

With this new hobby, the young eagle was able to look down from the blue sky instead of looking up into it. The sight from above was breathtaking and exciting.

Each day was a new day of unexplored challenges to the young eagle. The game of hide and seek with his 'brothers and sisters' no longer interested him. He would fly for hours, and when night came, he would return to the chicken coop. And the next day, he would get out and fly into the blue sky. The young eagle would do that day after day.

One wet and rainy day, the young eagle took shelter in an opening. In the rocky mountain with the father eagle. They were drenched as they waited for the rain to stop. Occasionally a bolt of lightning would strike across the dark sky, sending shivers through them. During a moment of silence, the father eagle spoke, "Young eagle, let me be frank with you. I have been watching your growth and progress and you have done well. But not well enough to be on your own."

"What do you mean not well enough to be on my own?" the young eagle asked.

"To be on your own, you need to detach yourself from the chickens, you need to stay away from them, the chicken coop is not your home, you are an eagle, not a chicken, and you certainly don't belong there. Here is where you belong," the father said philosophically.

Author's note:
No one can accomplish anything worthwhile if one mixes daily with losers. Winners like to do the things losers don't like to do, and losers like to do the things winners never want to do! Winners will not settle for less, nor would they want to come second. Whereas, losers don't mind where they are placed, they settle for leftovers.

You can't succeed if you hang around with losers, negative people, and people who have a poor life. So, detach yourself from those who are likely to pull you down, intentionally or unintentionally.

Hours passed. Desperate for further progress, the young eagle didn't wait for the rain to stop, he took a dive and vanished among the crowded bushes below. When he arrived at the chicken coop, it was almost the dawn of a new day.

The chickens asked him many questions, and he tried to answer them, for he had been with them for so long, they were like his own kin. He then said good-bye, and took off into the blue sky. He looked back for the last time. He could see his 'brothers and sisters' waving good-bye.

And for the first time in his life, he turned and said to the chickens, "Good-bye, you dirty looking chicken-shack, for you almost destroyed me. I am an eagle and you almost made me feel and act like a chicken. Good-bye, for I am not returning here any more…" And the eagle took off and found his freedom.

Author's note:
A time of realisation comes in everyone's life. When the time comes, the first important thing to do is to detach yourself from the losers. You need to literally tear yourself away from this lot of negative, put-down friends of yours. You may find it difficult to detach yourself from them in the beginning, and when you do, you may find yourself

bored, and lonesome. That is why you need to find substitutes. Before you detach yourself from this group of negative people you need to find a new group of positive people. You need to go out and make new friends. Joining clubs like the Rotary, Toastmasters, Lions, Jaycees or any club that promotes personal development and leadership is a good idea.

I have repeated the story of *The Day The Eagle Took Off* more than a 1000 times, in various institutions, corporations, government departments, and in all kinds of universities – in their conventions, seminars, workshops as well as in sales meetings in the past two decades. This classic piece of pep talk was nominated as the Motivational Seminar of the Year in 1994 by *Business Times*. It is one of my favourite short pep talks that gives the audience both a sense of worth and hope for a new beginning.

When one goes out in search of excellence, one must realise that there are certain principles that guide people to become successful in their respective fields. These principles are not my creation. When God was creating this world, he ordained these principles. Motivational gurus have passed down these and other principles to millions of people. I certainly hope you can follow some of them. Remember, I had stepped into the future with nothing, and came out as a winner, not because my parents left me millions of dollars in the bank. Nor was there a will in my name, left behind by a rich uncle somewhere. But because of the people who helped shape me, and the principles I applied, I was successful

THERE ARE

MANY CHAPTERS

IN ONE'S LIFE.

WHEN ONE IS OVER,

A NEW CHAPTER BEGINS

9

Success Principles

Principles are like a compass. When one is lost in the middle of nowhere, the only way out is to figure where you are at that point of time. Once you are able to identify where you are, then getting back to where you belong is easy. And one of the easiest ways to identify your location is by using a compass. Similarly, the principles for success guide us to greater success. Whether you like it or not, this is something you must rely upon...like the compass.

Success Principle #1

Change

"In order to keep growing day by day, we need to change...a change that will turn our world into a world of excitement and success."

Change

To succeed in life, one must learn to accept new things, and new changes. One may have been a very successful sales manager in the 60s; however, the techniques used in those days for handling people were different from the ones used today. Those days the sales manager could scream and shout at the salespeople. Today, the scene is totally different. Another scenario: a very bright student, with a superb high I Q who may have arrogantly accepted the highest honour, but, when it comes to his working life, he must learn to accept some changes, such as getting along with others who are not like himself, changes like working and going out with less intelligent people. He can no longer have the arrogant attitude he had during his campus days.

My specialty is recruiting. I run seminars on recruitment, and very often I am hired by sales organisations to conduct sales or business opportunity previews. The first thing one must have in mind when speaking in a business preview is being able to change the mindset of the listeners.

Remember, all who come to the seminar hall are brilliant and business-minded people. And your job, as required by your client, is to influence these business-minded people to make a change, hopefully, 'jump-camp' (switch to a new business opportunity). The speaker needs to be thinking ahead of these brilliant people, so it requires a certain amount of skill. To me, that's the easy part. All it needs is a few hours, and the job is done. But there is another change, which will take ages to accomplish. This involves developing certain attitudes in the individual. A better mental attitude will lead to a better individual. One of the more challenging jobs in my life as a speaker is to see a group of people walking into the seminar hall the first day, filled with all kinds of emotions, attitude and anxiety, and leaving, after 27 – 30 hours of endless tuning and attitudinal development, with a more positive approach to their daily work.

One of the most important studies in the recent years has been about change, about keeping up with the times. Toward the mid 90s, the IT world of dot com was introduced, and it is predicted that by the year 2003, if your company does not own a website, you will be classified backward in trends and in management. To me, that's change.

People, invariably don't like to change. They have learnt to like their way of doing things and become accustomed to specific habits, thinking patterns and way of life.

Perhaps, they are afraid of change. Some people are aware that their habits, thinking patterns and character traits are unsuitable and detrimental to success, but they still refuse to change. They do not want to do this because it requires commitment. It may mean more hard work or discipline or even letting go of something for which they have worked hard.

You may have had such experiences with older people. They stubbornly adhere to their own set of beliefs or practices and will not change at all. For instance, the father of a friend of mine was a heavy smoker and would light up a cigarette just about anywhere. His habit was to sit in the lounge after a meal smoking away his cigarettes. His children tried hard to get him to give up this disgusting habit for years, but he stubbornly refused, and eventually, his children gave up, despite their concern. And then, he was diagnosed with cancer, When he came home that day, he didn't sit in the lounge, rather, he sat with his children at the dinning table, talking to them. He gave up smoking the day he was diagnosed with cancer. What happened?

Change! The doctor had managed to change his mindset. Why couldn't his children do it? Authority makes the difference.

Today, younger people believe in progress, in getting ahead, and striving for something. And if there is a need to change, they will do so but not without a careful study of the pros and cons, the advantages and disadvantages involved.

Asians are generally very materialistic in their mindset. They strive hard to achieve more in life, and aspire for a better quality of life. Compared to Westerners, Asians are a more determined people. The five years I spent in Australia gave me better insight into the culture and lifestyle of the Australians. To the best of my knowledge, Asians in Australia tend to own two houses or more, whereas most Australians are content with one. It has often been asked, even in debates in universities, how Asians who have come to the country – some even by boat (the boat people) – were able to become owners of properties in such a short time.

I have two Vietnamese friends, who came to Australia some ten years ago. Today, one of them is the owner of a 7-storey building in the city of Sydney, from which he gets good returns from the rental alone. The other friend, has 16 units (apartments) all over Perth and New South Wales, and the rent he gets provides him a living. The more surprising thing is that many of these Asians only speak one language – their mother tongue.

Conclusion: The Australians have something to fall back on when things do not turn out right. They have a life-vest, (jacket) which can save them from drowning. Whereas the Asians will probably die in the ocean if they do not learn how to swim. So, the Asians ensure they get their butts out there to work hard daily.

When Asians come to Australia, in the beginning they have a different mindset from those already living there. The second and third generation Asians have another kind of mindset. They do not struggle as much as their forefathers did. They feel they do not need! Is it because they are brighter people? No, it is the system that makes them feel and think that way. The system has changed the mindset of these younger generations. Soon, the different Asian mindsets will eventually disappear in Australia. But as long as they keep on accepting people from Asia, its economy will be stable, because the new arrivals will strive hard to help keep the economy going.

No government in the world would want to feed people of another nationality, unless they are beneficial to them. That's why the immigration authorities of countries have guns and batons at their coasts these days, to keep immigrants out.

Basically, there are two kinds of change. When a decision to change is made, it is either out of audacity or fear. Both these elements are great motivators. Audacity enables looking out for more business opportunities, a better lifestyle and freedom. Fear makes you run away from certain authorities. My friend's father giving up the smoking habit was of course, motivated by fear. And the Asians who flock to Australia, looking for a better lifestyle and freedom are motivated by audacity.

A change motivated through audacity usually takes place when a person follows a programme or intensive workshop on personal development. He will be made aware of many things such as his weaknesses and strengths. He will then be encouraged to make some minor or major changes in order to improve his lifestyle.

Perhaps an individual doesn't believe in dressing-up for occasions because he does not feel the need for it. However, he may want to make some changes in his life by giving more importance to his attire because of certain motivating factors. It could be the need for freedom, security, love, and affection or simply the need to achieve recognition, self-assertion or self-actualisation.

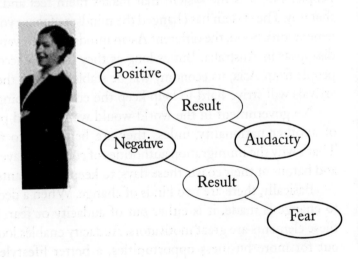

Incentives may motivate a person to higher levels of achievement and for that he may be willing to make changes in his life. But there is always room for improvement for, as the saying goes, nobody is perfect. Our era has shown an emphasis on progress and achievement and people have become more demanding in their quest for excellence.

First Change Your Thinking The Rest Of The Body Will Follow

If your desire is to succeed, then make some changes in your life. Remember, a winner does the things a loser doesn't like to do, while a loser does things that a winner doesn't like to do. If you choose to be a winner in life, then you need to make some changes, you have to stop doing some of the things which you have been doing, which can be detrimental in your life, which can become a stumbling block in your life. For example, you may need to stop going out with certain kind of 'close' friends whose behaviour is not conducive. Change if you want success... whatever the cost.

Success Principle #2

Belief

"If you plant in your subconscious mind the belief that you will be a success, you will harvest a great abundance of wealth and happiness."

Belief

As a young writer, whose mentor was Og Mandino, I met another very successful world-class author, M.R. Kopmeyer. His inspirational classics are *Here's How You Can Succeed*, and *Here's How You Can Get Anything You Want*. During a short session, he asked his students, "Just how do you know that you are capable of receiving the things you believe you will get?" As a mentor, Kopmeyer was fun and inspiring. He posed good questions and made his students think.

Let us go back to his question, "Just how do you know you are capable of receiving the things you believe you will get?"

If you believe in Nature's Universal Law of Cause and Effect just as you believe in the Law of Gravity, then you will get specifically what you believe in...intensely and not as a vague generality.

This is witnessed in the development of some of the richest people in the world, ranging from businessman Donald Trump; Malcolm Forbes, the founder of Forbes Magazine; Tan Sri Lim Goh Tong, the man behind the only official casino in Malaysia; Tan Sri Robert Kuok, the sugar king of the world; Rupert Murdoch, the creator of a world-wide media empire; Ted Turner, owner of CNN, the list can go on. They all had one common characteristic – belief in themselves. They believed they could, and they did achieve success! Nothing can hinder their belief in the things they want, and nothing is going to stop them if their minds are made up.

Let me tell you another secret of mine. It goes back to my first year as a labourer at the construction site in the city of Kuala Lumpur. There were times when the boss came to the site and instructed one or more workers to go to another site to work on some more important and urgent project.

Often, at the muddy construction site where we were hard at work, our shoes and legs would get filled with mud, dust or just plain cement. I had a really dirty pair of legs then.

Nothing Can Hinder

Your Thoughts

Nor Your Actions

If The Depth Of

Your Belief

Is Well Rooted

Deep Within You

There was an incident that I have never forgotten, whose impact was a lifelong one. My boss had instructed me, along with another worker, to go to a rich man's mansion to work on the roof tiles. We were given instruction on what to do and what not to do. We were told never to speak to the head of the house unless spoken to, and to whisper whenever we needed to communicate with each other. We were told to remain only at the place of work and not wander around the house, especially the swimming pool area. All instructions were properly read out, and we complied.

When we were driven to the posh mansion in Damansara Heights. I was amazed by the gigantic and magnificent building. It must have had some 10 rooms. I had never thought I would see a building like that anywhere in this world. Evidently, I was wrong!

"I wish one day to have a house like this," I told a fellow-worker. He burst out laughing. " You want to own a house like that? You got to be joking!"

"I believe I can," I told him while he shook his head in disbelief.

"Well, let's get into 'your house' now and see what needs to be done, David," he said. We took off our shoes, left them in the foyer, and headed straight to the back of the house. We made our way into the building, and were told of the problem by the housemaid.

Apparently, there was a leakage, and rainwater came gushing in when it rained. Then I was let into a room from where the maid had instructed that I could climb up into the attic through a tiny opening in the ceiling while another worker climbed onto the roof to examine it.

I was given a ladder and when I was making my way up the ladder, the owner's wife came into the room, and shouted, "How dare you come into the house with dirty feet?"

I got down from the ladder, lowered my head and apologetically I left the room to wash my feet and legs in the washing area. I had never thought that I would need to wash my feet to get into the attic. I was angry and frustrated... most of all I felt humiliated. But that's what I had to do, and I needed to complete the job. I felt that if could ever live in a house like this, my life would be perfect. I didn't think of how I could have the money to own a house of this size, but I just believed that I could, and I would, I must!

That incident occurred long ago. It is of no significance now, but its impact on me was so great. You may have come across the things you desire and want: do you dare to believe that one day you will?

Amazingly, not too many people dare to dream of things too big for them. Firstly, they don't see how they can get them and secondly, they don't believe that they deserve them!

They would rather live in a comfort zone, in the perimeter they are comfortable with; they dare not believe, maybe because they have not seen their own potential ability or simply don't want to take any chances, challenges or ventures! Stepping into the future with nothing means taking chances, challenges and venturing into a world of the unknown and unexplored. However, it all begins with "I believe I can!"

People Would Rather Live Within Their Comfort Zone – It Is A Size That Fits All

Begin today, adopt an attitude of believing in yourself and the things you want to achieve and attain in life. Begin with "I believe I can!" And with that, let it be known that nothing is ever going to stop you from further success, and no one is going to get in the way you are heading. Remember, your loved ones will probably give you a lot of resistance. You need to explain to them that the new challenge you are about to face is probably the best thing that is going to happen in your life, and that they should learn to accept you for what you are, for what you believe in, and for the journey you are about to embark on, ask for their support rather than fighting your way through. To go through the journey is already a challenge, and having them throw more challenges will jeopardise the entire episode.

Success Principle #3

The Goals In Life

"If you don't achieve anything by the time you approach 45, and you don't have a Goal that you can work for, chances are slim that you are ever going to make it."

Goals In Life

"What would you like to be when you grow up, David?" I was once asked. And I gave no answer, because, as a child, I never gave any importance to that issue. Unlike a friend of mine, who was asked the same question one day in school, and he said, "I would like to be a teacher." You know something, that statement was spoken some thirty years ago, and today that friend of mine is still in the teaching profession. Yes, if you put your heart, soul and mind into making something happen, something you really want, you will get it.

It was much later in life that I began to understand what goals are and their importance. It is most appalling to know that 95% of the people in the world drift aimlessly through life without the slightest perception of the work for which they are best suited, and with no feeling whatsoever of even the need of such a thing as a definite objective toward which to strive.

What is your definite, and chief aim in life? If I may ask...

Many people would find that question a bother. They would find it too troublesome even to think about it. What is your definite, chief aim in life? We see about us, on the ocean of life, young men and women aimlessly drifting, without rudder or port, killing time, without a definite purpose in anything they do. For they do not know what they are capable of, and their potential ability has never been put to use, so generally, they just wait...wait for something to happen.

Only some people take up challenges, and come out successful.

In 2001, I had the opportunity to meet, and share the platform with, Datuk Azhaar Mansor, the first Malaysian to sail alone around the world in 1999. The trip took him some 190 days on board his *jelur germilang*. I am pretty sure that Datuk Azhaar Mansor didn't wake up one morning and decide that he would jump into his boat and bid his family good-bye for a trip around the world. The trip must have been carefully and painstakingly planned, and every detail must have been carefully thought about much before the day he bid everyone good-bye.

Planning

Most people I know love to dream. Many of them dare to dream, but only a small number go to the extent of planning for a dream. Planning your dream is the first step toward greater success in whatever you do. Most of the students who come to my seminars over the year will agree with me when I say that most of us dare to dream, but not many of us put the dream into its planning stage. Why? Is your dream of any significance to your livelihood? If the dream is not your top priority, you won't bother to think about it. I call it daydreaming.

Let's talk about planning. The first part of goal setting is to have a dream, a dream that is of some significance in your life. The dream must have an impact that changes your entire life.

I am often hired to speak at annual functions by various clients. My objective for the day or the evening is to sell a dream. Some 60 – 150 people come to the function each time. You have probably attended such a function. Yes, that's the network-marketing business. In such business sessions, I sell dreams to people. I have spoken on Forever Living Products, Herbal Life, Nu Skin, Amway, AIM, just to name a few, and you know what's so amazing about these functions? I see the same old faces at each of these meetings. The same individuals go to different meetings and because of their attendance, I get to know some of them personally. The fascinating thing about these people is that they are just 'looking out for the perfect dream." Amazingly enough, some of them have been looking for the perfect dream ever since we brought in the concept of network marketing some 30 years ago and they still haven't found one. However, I must admit there are also hundreds who have found their dream. Yes, I sincerely urge you to get a dream, and make it your own dream! Then comes the part of planning.

As I have said earlier, many people love to dream. Since this is the first part of goal setting, let's do a little exploration here. No matter who you are, or where you have been, we have all one way or another, had the opportunity to do some planning in our lives. There are two kinds of planning that I know of. The first one is known as 'subconscious planning,' and the other is 'blueprint' planning. I will now explain the difference in results between these two kinds of planning.

Subconscious Planning

The average person who is struggling to succeed in life may have found a dream but will apply only subconscious planning. He is not serious enough to make it a reality. It is a dream based on fascination or idealism, but not reality. The dream has little impact for he would, at any time, forgo or compromise the dream for something else.

Subconscious planning is not a good thing. It destroys rather than builds; it wears you out so quickly that before you know it, you are already talking about another dream. That's why you have so many people who swear to the effectiveness of a product and, much later, they sell you another kind.

Blueprint

The word applies to the people who know how to plan consciously and begin shaping the plan into reality. We call this a blueprint. It is the very first step towards achieving your dream. Without this blueprint, there is no way you can arrive at the point of success. I would like to carefully take you through the steps in my blueprint for your success. No, I seriously don't think you should skip this segment of this chapter. Yes, you may say that you have sat through hundreds of goal-setting sessions. I am thankful you have done that, for it will only make my work a little easier. Now, just one more time, and I am going to ensure that this time, it is going to be worthy, because there are certain components that are very important and need to be addressed.

Component In Blueprint

Each of our dreams must have a name for you to relate to. Many of our dreams are without a name. That's not possible! If a dream goes without a name, it is like a man without a name. You need to have a name, whether it is generic or specific, it really doesn't matter much, so long as you are able

I'm gonna get you!

to relate to the name of your dream. I have a number of generic names for certain dreams of mine.

Name Your Dream

For instance the three books that I needed to complete in 1994, were called 3 Sellers. Here's another one, Peak-World. I remember the time when I was just starting out in my speaking career, and I wanted to hit the big time, I wanted so much to be able to speak to audiences around the globe, and Peak-World was the name given to that dream.

A statement of conviction must be written just below the name of your dream. It is a statement that will push you constantly, relentlessly, and forcefully.

After the statement of conviction has been identified, comes the part of dating the exercise. There will always be a

---

Peak-World

Sharing your message of importance with audiences around the world. Starting with Asia

| 8th July 1981 | through | 8th July 1983 |

beginning and a date for accomplishment. It doesn't matter if you need to take four months or four years to realise your dream, but it must be established. Given in the previous page is my 16cm x 8cm blueprint.

As you may have realised, computers and the world of IT hadn't really taken a toll then, and therefore, I embossed the word, 'Peak-World' by tracing the letters out from an old newspaper and typed the statement of conviction and the date of starting and accomplishing neatly, on my faithful old typewriter.

Constant Reminder

I duplicated the words 'Peak-World' by a photocopier, several copies were made and I pasted them all over my house, from the bathroom mirror to the side of the toilet roll. I pasted them in the living-room, storeroom and bedroom. I pasted them on the dashboard of my car, and on my office drawer. I would be reminded daily of the blueprint when I opened my briefcase. When you are reminded daily about your dream, you begin to work for it. Your mind automatically goes to work with the best knowledge you have stored. You will soon begin to see yourself networking for that very purpose.

If you ask me about the result, I must say the result was astonishing. By the time I returned from New York, after spending nearly two years there (1985 and 1986) I was convinced that our goals in life are a lot easier to achieve if we put them down on paper.

Action

Today, as an author, I am constantly writing. I spend countless hours in front of my personal computer in the privacy of my bedroom. Sometimes without stepping out for two to three days. I have a refrigerator in my bedroom; it is well stocked with chocolate bars, cookies and other sources of inspiration that also give a full stomach. A coffee maker is in the pantry at the corner of my bedroom. Yes, I am well stocked! Judy reminds me about lunch or dinner, and sometimes I have my meals at the study table in the bedroom itself. Now there is a poster on my bedroom wall. On it, are clearly printed the words that have been spoken by every motivational speaker in the world. "The greatest thing in this world is not so much where we are, but in what direction we are moving." One common thing among writers is the time we spend 'lost in space'. I could be sitting there for two hours and not a single word is typed, at least three cups have been consumed, still nothing happens! The poster is hung in such a way that it reminds me to get on with my writing whenever I find myself 'lost in space.'

The little episode above explains the action part of the blueprint, if you want to achieve anything in life – yes, literally everything! Yes, you can, provided you put in the effort. Action is the most important part of your goal. Get onto it right away, not tomorrow, nor when the kids get home, but right away.

Challenges

I have four daughters, Deniese, Debbie, Denissa and the youngest, Delena. They come in and interrupt my writing at times, and that's one of the challenges I get from my writing. Patiently I attend to their needs and get on with my writing again. At times I feel frustrated because of the lack of concentration, or missing out a point in certain modules. But I can't blame my children for it. I know they miss their dad, they want me to play with them, they want my attention.

Handling The Challenges

So, I had to figure a better way to overcome this. Now whenever they need to talk to me, I stop them for a few seconds by saying, "Wait! Just a second…" Then I type some jargon on the computer screen that will remind me of the point that I want to prove when I continue later.

Yes, for every goal you set, there will be challenges. The challenges I faced in writing books are really no big deal compared to some of you whose dreams are so much greater than mine. But the point I am trying to establish here is that every goal has its challenges. Just handle one challenge at a time; long term planning can ease short-term frustrations.

Visualisation (act as if ...)

This may sound a little arrogant, but I normally get to see the finished product even before my dream is realised. Here is the reason why, as you know, my goals revolve around the writing of books.

Before the writing is completed, I have the advertising agency come up with a mock copy of the book, illustrating the title of the book, the photographs, captions and reviews. I get to see the finished copy of the book before it is sent to my publisher.

I would like to share with you another theory of visualisation. I longed to own a Jaguar ever since I started out as a salesman of a magazine. One day I was invited to a party, and in the midst of chatting with friends, I saw a Jaguar pull up in front of my friend's house. It was a slick-looking car, very spacious and elegant. A young man alighted from the car "Who is that?" someone asked. "That's George Devan, a very successful life insurance agent!" another answered. From that point onward, owning a Jaguar became a passion, and that dream kept me going for at least some 20 years. When I could afford it, I went after it like a leopard!

However, in your case, you can visualise your dream by seeing yourself as the person who has had success in whatever your dream is all about.

If your dream is about financial success, then I think you should go to a photo studio and have a photograph taken of yourself wearing a tuxedo. Or simply go and stand next to an

S or E Class Mercedes to have your picture taken. Get copies of it, and put these in the places you are most likely to visit daily. See it, feel it and act as if you already have it!

Review

In everything we do, there must be checks and balances. You need to examine yourself and review your own progress. See how far you have gone, and how close you are to the goal you set. There is a phrase I learned a long time ago: "If you expect something to turn out good, then you must inspect what you expect." The last thing you want to do is to leave your goal unchecked. No matter how close you are to your goal, if you don't review it, you will never know what has been done and what hasn't. Recently, I attended a programme conducted by Time System, which has been extremely helpful for me personally. Since that day, I rarely leave home without my personal diary, and hardly a day goes by without my reviewing what has been done during that day.

Temporary Goal Vs Long Term Frustration

So many people make the same mistake time and again: setting a temporary goal, with long-term frustration. You may have seen this yourself. A new sales agent, or salesman whose career was about to take off, everything seemed to be going okay, then he went on to buy an expensive automobile that doubled his burden. This is the scenario.

Murdock, a life insurance agent, was recruited a year ago. He came into the industry with good intentions, wanting to make it good in his new career. Diligently, Murdock went to work daily with discipline. He called on every prospective client he knew; soon, he was making some progress. One day, he was in a sales convention and he got a lift with his agency manager to the venue. The agency manager owned an E class Mercedes that cost something like RM300,000. Naturally, he was inspired when he stepped into this world-class vehicle. The smell of the leather left a lasting impression on him and the touch-buttons on the dashboard evoked Murdock's admiration. "You need to own one of these…" The agency manager said. "Makes you look successful, clients trust you more," he went on.

That night, Murdock couldn't sleep although he was exhausted after a day of listening to the various speakers at the conference. His mind was racing, he wanted to own an E Class' as well.

Murdock woke up the next morning with great anticipation. He went to the agency manager and told him of his dream, wanting to take his advice on how to become the proud owner of an E Class Mercedes. The agency manager felt good because he had successfully motivated Murdock to take this course of action.

With all his savings, and a little help from his in-laws, Murdock got his brand new E Class in the next three months. The monthly repayment was something like RM9,000 per month for the next seven years. There wasn't much of a challenge to maintain that repayment scheme.

However, in 1997, everything came to a standstill when the world economy slow-down hit the Malaysians. Murdock's income also came to a standstill, nobody was buying, everyone was restricting their spending. Three months went by without a cent given to service the interest of the vehicle. The fourth schedule was issued by the finance company: if there was no payment they would take action in the next 21 days, to retrieve the vehicle from Murdock. Poor Murdock was desperate, and for the first time in his life he was scared. He tried to hide the car, but it was too big a vehicle to hide, and the thought of losing the car increased Murdock's frustration.

To cut the story short, Murdock lost the E class, he lost everything and today he is out of business. He is working as a salesman in a computer company, selling computers as a shop assistant.

Don't live in this kind of dream. As a matter of fact it was a nightmare. Just imagine, what motivation did the car give? It was nothing but a burden! A vehicle like an E Class was never meant to be an inspiration. The people who can afford to drive around in a car like that have money working for them. It is certainly not meant for salespeople who are striving toward making progress.

I love the Jaguar, but I didn't own it until I could afford it. I just didn't want my ultimate dream to be affected in any way. If you are under financial constraints, what possibilities are there for you to succeed? You can't! Because half the time you are so bogged down with financial worry, you can't concentrate on what you do best. Don't live a life with a temporary dream that leads to long-term frustration.

Success Principle #4

Learn The Art of Personal Selling

*"If you get too comfortable with your
job, then, it is time that
you learn to sell."*

The Art of Personal Selling

Selling is the highest-paid profession in the world. This is the first statement I will expound in my two-day sales workshop, entitled: *The Making Of A Super Salesperson.* Whether you are a bank officer, or an executive trying to sell your boss a new success plan, or a clerk whose job is about filing and keeping records, no matter who you are, you should learn the art of personal selling. Until you learn the art of personal selling, you are not going to acquire much more than you already have, because personal selling is about higher attainment in life, it is about achieving more in life. If you are content with the way things are, happy with what you have, and satisfied with what you get...a mere mediocre, then, this is not the book for you.

Why is personal selling so important?

Let me put it this way. If you want something in life, there are only two ways to get it: either you demand it, which is going to piss everybody off, or you can sell your idea and get it. The same is true for marriage, both parties must learn the skill of communication (selling) or the marriage will end up with hypertension, which subsequently will lead to separation. A child should also learn the art of asking (selling to) elders and for students too, this skill needs to be acquired.

When you learn the art of personal selling, you will realise that people willingly give you the things you want. Let me take you through a simple step in personal selling.

Just how do you get someone to willingly give you the things you ask for? Take for instance, my youngest daughter, Delena. She loves all kinds of potato chips, and whenever we go shopping, she nags us to buy her favourite chips. Judy and I felt she was having too much of these, so we came up with an idea, and started selling her the disadvantages of eating too many potato chips.

I came up with a story of a friend's daughter who had too many potato chips and as a result, became so fat, that her parents had a hard time getting her into the car. Each time Delena heard this story, she would forget the idea of buying the potato chips.

What makes Delena waive the idea of pursuing the subject? She didn't want to end up like the girl I had described, isn't it? Now, that is personal selling to some extent. Because I had successfully sold the idea to Delena that potato chips were not good for her and would make her fat, she gave them up.

One must learn this approach to get the things we want in life. Stop yelling for the things you want and start selling your way through.

The first thing you ought to understand about personal selling is the effect of benefits. Everybody is looking for benefit of some kind. Why do we go to work daily? Because we want to earn the money to buy the things we need, and money is the benefit in this standpoint. Why do you send your kids for

tuitions? You want your kids to stay on the cutting edge and be brighter students, so being brighter is the benefit that accrues when you send them to those tuition classes.

Why do people jam their way through a crowded city just to buy something? To buy that 'something' is their benefit. Now, unless you are that someone who would jam his way through the crowded city, you can't see the benefit. That's why we can't understand why some people do certain things, which might look silly to you. They have a reason, they see benefit in it.

The skill here is to help others see the benefit, and when they do, they will buy, no matter how worthless or worthy it may be, they will go ahead and buy it. That's personal selling.

Once you understand people's intentions and the benefits they are after, you will know how to sell your way to their hearts.

There is a difference between FM Radio and AM Radio. Both work the same way except for the wave each carries, the difference is in how the carrier wave is modulated. With AM Radio, the amplitude, or overall strength, of the signal is varied to incorporate the sound information. Whereas in FM, the frequency (the number of times each second the current changes direction) of the carrier signal is varied.

FM signals have an advantage over AM signals. Both signals are susceptible to slight changes in amplitude. With an AM broadcast, these changes result in static. With an FM broadcast, slight changes in amplitude don't matter at all. Since the audio signal is conveyed through changes in frequency, the FM receiver can simply ignore the changes in amplitude.

The final result; no static at all.

Now, within us, we have an FM receiver, and we call it WIIFM. Everyone owns an FM receiver, and all we have to do is understand how the carrier wave is modulated, then we will have something in common. Let's explore the radio station within us further...

People Do Things
For Their Own Benefit
Everyone Is Out There
Looking For Benefits

WIIFM

The FM Radio Station known as WIIFM stands for: **W**hat's **I**n **I**t **F**or **M**e. Like in any business deal, there is a buyer and a seller. The seller needs to understand the buyer's needs, and if the seller can identify the needs then the business deal will be closed without much interruption. The unfortunate ones keep telling and not selling. You can't get much out of telling, but through selling, you can get everything! The important thing is to find out what the other fellow wants! Evidently, everyone wants benefit. Everyone is out there looking for some kind of benefits. And if we can provide the benefit they are looking for, then we have something in common.

Many a time, when coaching younger salespeople in their sales interviews, I have witnessed that the inexperienced salespeople tend to ask for the sale before they have really understood what the buyers are looking for.

"If you have not established what the buyers' benefits are, don't go further. Search for clues for what the buyers want!" I said to these young salespeople.

Think about this for a while, why did people line up for hours to buy the *Hello Kitty* collections when McDonalds launched the promotion? The newspapers reported that some Singaporeans fought their way to the counter, and some had heated arguments. Some even got involved in brawls for that event.

Dreadful? Ridiculous? Silly?

No, not to those who saw the benefits they were going after. To some of us, it was a ridiculous event. I mean, how could anyone line up for hours just for the *Hello Kitty* collections?

The older generation would be appalled to see people lining up for an hour trying to buy a ticket for a show in the Cineplex. Benefits! Everyone is looking for benefits. Each of us wakes up every morning looking for some kind of benefits. I wake up at 4.00 am daily looking for my benefit, and that's the quiet moment that I can have for my writings and research work while my kids are still asleep.

Once the benefits are established, you will get what you want. I suggest that you read my book *The Making of A Super Salesperson.* In it you will discover more selling skills. The five rules of selling (from attention to probing, leading, assurance and close) are also written for this purpose.

Don't be content with your present way of life. Take a lesson from this old buddy. Learn the art of personal selling. Better still, get involved in some kind of networking business or become a life insurance agent. In recent years, the life insurance industry had been very kind to me, I have had the opportunity to share my thoughts and wisdom with many life insurance agents all over this country as well as overseas. During these tours, I have had the privilege to meet some of the most eminent agents in the business.

Every year, I have been a guest speaker at their annual convention, and I have seen many ordinary people doing extraordinary things. Women who had been cooking in the kitchen all their lives, attending to the laundry and household chores, waiting patiently for their husbands to return home, were given a chance to learn the art of personal selling. These women took advantage of the skill and some went on to become the most eminent life insurance agents in the industry.

ORDINARY PEOPLE

DOING EXTRAORDINARY THINGS

YOU CAN BE TRAINED

TO BE EXTRAORDINARY!

Learn the art of personal selling. Don't be a hypocrite! Get involved in some kind of buying and selling business. Stop saying, "Selling is not for me, or I really don't need the money!" People who say they don't need the money are actually lying to themselves as well as to others. Not too long ago, I was invited to speak at the annual convention of a network marketing company in the Philippines. They were honouring the most outstanding distributors of the year. Like any other annual convention, there were speeches galore. When it was the turn of the distributor of the year to share his thoughts, we were asked to stand up as he made his entrance. My first reaction was that this was another of those network-marketing stances for recognising the same old distributor whose ego had been blown out of proportion, but I stood up along with the rest.

To my amazement, the distributor who came on the stage to share his thoughts that evening was a newcomer.

"I never knew selling was for me. I was wrong, and I had been wrong all these years. I became a distributor with this company last year, and I started selling their products only some nine months ago. I just kept selling, sponsoring and more selling and...." True to his words, this newcomer earned more than he had earned in his entire career as a mechanic in a motorcycle workshop in a remote suburb of Manila.

In my records, there are well over a thousand testimonies of life insurance agents and networking distributors who have done well in their lives.

The average people will stay average because they refuse to give themselves a chance to learn the art of personal selling. Many don't see themselves as being able to, because they don't want to be branded as another salesperson hassling others for a living. Some just don't know what to do and how to do it and I don't blame them. I was also just another fellow who thought selling was really not for me. If I hadn't got involved with *Time Magazine* decades ago, I wouldn't be what I am today.

The truth of the matter is, we don't really need to hassle others into buying from us. Personal selling is about skill, and if you can learn this skill, not only can you sell a tangible product and earn lots of money, you can also sell wisdom and other values to your loved ones at home.

A big Yes to personal selling!

Success Principle #5

Burning Desire

"Unless you have the burning desire to succeed, all the dreams in the world mean nothing."

Burning Desire

My recent trip to Chicago proved to be a worthwhile one. I had breakfast at a café that early winter morning with my good friend, Jimmy Johnson who shared with me the lesson of desiring something badly, and I thought it was so beautifully shared – and it would be a waste if I don't share it with you.

The morning after the great Chicago Fire, a group of merchants stood on State Street, still shocked by the devastating event that had wiped out everything. They began discussing whether they should rebuild Chicago, or move somewhere else. All of them decided to relocate except one who decided to stay on and told the others, " Gentlemen, on this very spot, I will build the world's greatest store, no matter how many times it may burn down, no matter how many times I have to build it again and again…" That was more than 100 years ago. Today, Marshall Fields still stand proudly on State Street in Chicago.

Desire – burning desire. According to Napoleon Hill's classic *Think and Grow Rich*, we learn that: thoughts are things, that have tangible and measurable substance to them and thought is the fundamental building block for success. The world conforms perfectly to our thoughts, be they weakening and destructive or lofty and empowering. I would like to draw your attention to this elevated principle of desire.

Without desire, all the other principles that we are discussing in this book become meaningless, and insignificant. This principle of desire is the only creative power behind all manifestation. It has been said that nothing can be achieved without a burning desire. If you stop to analyse it long enough, you will agree that nothing that you have ever achieved has happened without this white heat of desire behind it. Desire is not 'wishing,' 'hoping' or just a mere 'wanting.' We have all wanted something in our lives, but nothing came of it.

There is a little game I deploy whenever I am invited to speak on the topic of motivation. I grab a copy of my book or sometimes a whole set of books, and holding it in my hand, I ask the audience, "This set of books costs something like $100. Now, how many of you in this room would like to have them for free?"

Thoughts Are The Fundamental Building Blocks For Greater Success

Normally, I will see some twelve people putting up their hands to show their desire, and on my asking a few more times, more hands go up in the air, and finally, someone staggers up to grab those books from my hands. "That's what I mean by action! Desire is about action, not wishing, hoping or just wanting to obtain the things we want in life!"

Desire consumes one with a single-mindedness that borders on obsession. It focusses our thoughts very much like a magnifying glass focusses sunlight to create fire. Desire develops within us the confidence that what we seek is possible. As our desire increases, the possibility of achieving what we want is greater. If thoughts are the vehicle of our creation, then desire is the fuel that pushes the vehicle forward. If we do not sufficiently desire a thing, then the first sign of resistance we face, will often make us turn away from the goal. Only a desire of sufficient intensity will cause us to remain committed to our dreams.

The world stopped working on the morning of 11 September 2001 to witness the relentless replay on CNN of the Twin Towers in New York being torn down by two aeroplanes.

Do Not Ask Yourself

If You Deserve It,

Do Not Succumb To Temptation

And Prevent Yourself

From Getting It.

Develop An Insatiable Desire

To Get The Things

God Has Promised

My wife and I shed tears as we watched the victims being carried out. We felt further hurt when the families of those victims came on air to voice their sadness and desperation. When the President of United States, George W Bush went to the site – Ground Zero – to comfort those who were grieving, our sadness was given a ray of hope. The people wanted to see justice done, and his only desire then was to ensure that justice is done. No matter what it takes and how long it takes – justice will be done! Weeks went by, and turned into months. American soldiers were stationed in Afghanistan pounding away at those responsible for the massacre on the morning of September 11th. They spent billions of dollars on this war with Osama bin Laden. Here is a classic example of desire displayed by the American people.

Desire. When you burn with an insatiable desire to achieve your goal, do not be surprised at the looks of disdain from those around you. Look at Marconi, the radio inventor, who was advised by his friends to look for professional help, and subsequently he was put into a mental institution when he announced to the world that he had discovered the means by which he could send messages through the air, without wires. You don't need to look so far; look at the people who laughed at me when I told them I wanted to be a writer. These were people whom I thought were my friends, they seemed so caring; in the early days, they provided so much good advice, but, when I announced to them my intention, they laughed cynically.

My desire was strong and crystal clear and I went after my goal without letting go and never wanting to let go. In 1995-1996, one of my books *52 Ways To Make More Money In Network Marketing* sold more than one million copies, that shut up everybody once and for all! However, let me repeat, I am not talking about mere 'wishing.' Remember, he who merely wishes, does not believe that he will achieve what he wishes for.

It matters not what your dream is. If your desire is total and complete, nature will bend to your will and that dream will materialise for you. Edison, Carnegie, Wilbur, Datuk Azhaar Mansor, Donald Trump, and many other greats used this same principle.

Think of the time in your own life when you burned with a desire to have something. Maybe it was a new home, a new car, a job that you desperately needed, or a relationship. Something that was so important to you and nothing was going to stand in the way of attaining it. You need to harness the same deeply held desire that caused you to do whatever it took to attain that which you fervently desired in the past, and apply it in the present.

Whatever it is that you desire in life, make that desire burn deeply within your soul. Do not question its worth. Do not ask yourself if you deserve it or not. Do not succumb to the temptation to minimise it, because it is something that you want, ardently want! Flame that white heat of desire into an obsession and tell yourself that nothing is going to stand in your way. Nothing is going to stand between you and its achievement. Want it enough; it will surely be yours.

Success Principle #6

Expectation

"To expect...
you need to inspect!"

Expectation

"That evening when I left my house in Vietnam, I knew life would be different. I expected to live a happier life, and a more complete one. Without fear and without having to look for shelter. Today, that expectation has granted me much more than I had asked for," Leroy related to me.

Leroy Lam, a Vietnamese, came to Sydney, Australia, some 30 years ago. He was 36 years old. When he came to Australia, he had nothing. He had traded all his assets in Vietnam for a better life in Australia.

Leroy and his wife, Kuan, left Vietnam on a September night in 1970, in a big boat that was crammed with some 80 others.

"We took along with us rice and two bags of potatoes. Hidden in my belt were some gold ingots that were worth something like $60,000 today."

He had intended to buy a lease of life in Australia with those gold ingots.

"We must have been drifting for days in the South China Sea, when we were told that a boat was approaching us. To our dismay, our greatest fear came true – pirates. David, all my gold ingots were taken away, and for the rest of the trip, Kuan cried. All I could do was comfort her."

When they landed in Australia, Leroy and Kuan were taken to a huge centre that provided shelter for all the 'boat-people'. "The pride within us vanished the very moment we landed in Australia. We knew from the very beginning that we needed to be obedient and follow instructions and not get into trouble. No pride but lots of expectation. We were anxious to get out of the centre, to get a job and begin life…" Kuan added.

Today, Leroy and Kuan own three shops in Chinatown in Sydney, and their home in Castle Hills has a million-dollar view of the city. Both their children are now working.

The key word in my interview with Leroy was: *Expectation.*

Expectation – what is this source of energy? Expectation is nothing more than a ray of hope we carry with us.

How many times in our lives have we been put in such a position? And just how many times have your expectations turned out to be exactly as you had expected? There are basically two types of expectation. One, of course, is the positive expectation and the other is the opposite. Both these expectations give you the same portion of what you expect. The energy directed by your thoughts will eventually turn into action.

That is why you should, at all times, add precautions to your expectations. Avoid the energy being directed from a negative standpoint, because the result will be devastating.

When I was a salesman selling cookware, I met a lady whom I would describe as a most negative individual. Although she appeared to be kind and friendly, deep within, this poor old soul was extremely negative in all aspects of her life.

She complained about almost everything I was promoting, from the handle of the cookware to the five-ply underneath the cookware. The colour wasn't right, the packaging did not suit her taste. Then she went on to complain about her neighbours. "If they don't lock up their dogs, some day, somebody is going to get killed!"

Your guess is right! Miss Jenny never bought my set of cookware, and I never went back to see her again. Several months later, my colleague told me that Miss Jenny had passed away.

You may also have met people who are like this, who live in a world of negative expectations. They are mostly miserable and tired looking. They seldom get along with people, and most people do not welcome them either.

Avoid this energy coming from the negative standpoint. If you expect the negative, it will prevail. The king of rock 'n roll, Elvis Presley's mother Gladys, died at the young age of 43. Elvis was very close to his mother when she died, according to Donna Presley Early, Elvis's first cousin whom I had the opportunity to meet during my tour of Canada in 1999. "It was 3.00 am on August 13th, 1958 when Elvis received a call from Vernon that he should come to the hospital right away. When he got there, Gladys was gone. And from that day onwards, Elvis was never the same. He had no direction, he was adrift, no goal, no fun to be with. Often, Elvis would say 'I would give up everything...if it would bring mama back again'."

Talking about negative expectation, when Elvis died at the age of 43, it made headlines in every newspaper around the world. For it was the prime of his life, and it shocked the world! According to some psychologists Elvis Presley's negative expectations hastened his death.

If you direct this energy from a positive standpoint, many wonderful things will take place. Your life will be better, your world will be a better place to live in. Everything in your surroundings will look brighter and better. Expect goodness, and goodness shall flourish. However, my research has proved that with every good expectation there are challenges, a sort of relentless trial – a testing moment – you may like to call it.

Expect Goodness, And Goodness Shall Flourish

For this Mother Nature has instilled a great force of relentless trial whenever a good expectation is applied. A good expectation must come with a relentless trial because it adds greater meaning, strength, and most of all a valuable significance to the expectation. After all, good expectation is not really a gift from Mother Nature; we are supposed to develop it ourselves. Having good expectations is like developing muscles in our body, it is a day-to-day affair. We can't go to a gymnasium just for one day and walk out, looking like the guy you saw in '*Terminator II.*'

Since the beginning of time every, prophet, scholar, scientist, inventor, singer, writer, celebrity and great businessman has had one thing in common, and that is, whenever they apply this law of good expectations, invariably they are tested, invariably they go through relentless trial before their objective is finally achieved. Most of these greats met their greatest challenge in their pursuit of excellence.

You have probably read about the amazing Cyrus Field, a retired successful businessman who came up with the idea that telegraphic communication could be established between Europe and America through cable at the bottom of the Atlantic Ocean. Let's look at the preliminary work which included the construction of a telegraph line one thousand miles long, from New York to St. John's, Newfoundland. Through four hundred miles of almost unbroken forest, they had to build a road as well as a telegraph line across Newfoundland. Another stretch of one hundred and forty miles across the island of Cape Breton involved a great deal of labour, as did the laying of a cable across the St. Lawrence.

For every mile of cable laid, Cyrus Field met the challenges, and unremittingly, he faced them all, one at a time. He worked hard to secure aid for his company from the British Government, but in the US Congress he encountered major opposition. For every successful moment, Cyrus faced yet another challenge. The challenges kept coming, as his expectation grew.

The cable was loaded upon the *Agamemnon*, the flagship of the British fleet at Sebastopol and upon arriving at the Niagara, on a magnificent new frigate of the US Navy. But, when five miles of cable had been laid, it got caught in the machinery and broke. Another challenge: two hundred miles at sea, and the electricity current was suddenly lost. Cyrus and his men paced the decks nervously and sadly. " We should just pack up and go home…" one man said to another. Cyrus Field heard this, came up to the man, grabbed him by his collar, and this is what he said, "I expect this dream of mine to be fulfilled, and no one in my team is going to give up and get in my way. Now is the time to inspect what has gone wrong, it is not the time to pack up and go home!" Then the electricity current was restored, and the following night, when the ship was moving at a speed of four miles an hour, and the cable was running out at the rate of six miles, the brakes were applied too suddenly just as the ship gave a heavy lurch, and the cable broke again.

Cyrus Field was not one to give up so easily. "Let's order another seven hundred miles of cable, and give me another set of men of great skill," he ordered his company. This time,

American and British inventors united in making this dream a reality. In mid-ocean, the two halves of the cable were spliced and the steamers began to separate. One headed for Ireland, and the other for Newfoundland, each running out the precious thread, which, it was expected, would bind two continents together.

Before the vessels were three miles apart, the cable broke – another challenge! Again it was spliced, this time when the vessels were eighty miles apart; again the electricity current was lost.

The directors were disheartened, the public sceptical, the capitalists were hesitant, and the men at the deck disappointed, all except one, Cyrus Field. " We have come this far, if I have to die to see this become a reality, I will! Let's get back to work!"

A third attempt was made. The entire cable was laid without a break, and several messages were flashed through nearly seven hundred leagues of ocean, when suddenly, Mother Nature appeared with another test, and the electricity current ceased again. Tears rolled down the cheeks of every man who was involved in this great project of Cyrus Field who had lost his entire fortune in this expedition. Feeling distressed, he went down on his knees and prayed to God, "I don't need more cables now, I need strength from You..."

Cyrus Field went to work again. Persuading investors to provide the capital. He faced rejection from all quarters. Finally, he organised a new company, and made a new cable, far superior to anything used before, and on 13th July 1866, the cable was laid in perfect working order.

The greater expectation one has, the greater the challenge there is...

Success Principle #7

Take Responsibility

"At the end of everything,
there's a word:
Accountability!"

Take Responsibility

At the end of everything, you are answerable for your actions. That's taking responsibility! Stop passing the buck and get a life! That's what every corporate figure wants his employee to do.

Take a look around you, why is there so much misery and unhappiness in the workplace as well as in our personal lives? People blame each other and when the blaming game begins, productivity slows down. As you may know, the blaming game goes on in every corporation, at every level from the tea lady to the receptionist, and from the errand-boy to the security guard. If that's not enough, let's look at the secretaries of some of the departmental heads; many of them go to work with the intention of crucifying someone that day. Inevitably, most of them will swear before their CEOs that there is no such thing going on around in the office, and the CEOs will prefer to pretend that there is no game of this nature. But the truth is...there is.

As a corporate trainer as well as a consultant, I have sat in many corporate and management meetings as well as senior management meetings. I have seen managers of various departments blaming each other for the decrease in sales or some other crisis in the office. When the sales department is not performing well, the sales manager blames the marketing department for not creating enough awareness, and the marketing department blames it on the insufficient funds received from the finance department, and the finance department shoots back at the sales and marketing department for their incompetence, and while the CEO looks for an answer to end all this, the human resource manager stands up and says "I really think we got the wrong people for the job!" It's like a circle in there.

When You Blame Others,
You Blame Yourself

People are quick to blame others; they search for a scapegoat the moment something goes wrong. These are people that make 95% of the corporate-ladder striving mongrels. And you know something? They are not going to get there if they continue to carry with them a load of excuses. People must learn to stop blaming others and take responsibility for their actions.

However, I have been to meetings in some corporations where everyone is accountable for their actions. If the sales department is not doing well, the marketing department works with the finance department to come up with a proper solution to help increase the sales in the following months. This could mean increasing the budget for advertising in the mass media or working closely with the human resource department to hire more sales people. Successful managers look for an avenue or an angle to solve a crisis while the incompetent look for a way out by blaming others.

The same rule applies in personal development. We will not grow if we keep on blaming others for our failures. When things go wrong, as they sometime will, we must first learn the rule of nature; *when you blame others, you blame yourself.* It simply means that when you begin blaming someone, you are, in fact, blaming yourself. However, I really don't blame those who are so quick to blame others when something goes wrong! Because, this is the very first lesson a young child learns!

Elders teach us to protect ourselves in the first few lessons of life, and many of us misunderstand the term 'protection' and use it as 'excuses.' Therefore, when excuses are needed, the term 'blame' will naturally appear before us. We think that when we blame others, we are, in fact, protecting ourselves. On the contrary, when things go wrong and when you become the victim of circumstances, then, you are required to protect yourself by reasoning out who and what's right!

Success Principle #8

Thriftiness

"At the age of 55,
if you are still flat-broke...
you will begin to wonder
why you had spent money on
those unnecessary items earlier."

Thriftiness

The year 2002 was a great one for me. The year started and ended with a national speaking tour with one of the biggest unit trust companies in Malaysia. With these two national speaking tours, I was convinced that the country was really gearing up for the greatest 'lesson' in life.

The Art of Saving Money

During my tour I came to understand that most urban wage earners would earn something like RM1-1.5 million in their entire life. For a country like Malaysia, I would say the standard of living is pretty healthy and the lifestyle great. Our children get most of the things they want and we tend to pamper ourselves with many wonderful things in life.

On the other hand, in my 25 years as a speaker and trainer, I have seen many who have retired but are still struggling with another job. When asked why they still needed a job, most of them would say, "can't afford not to..." and you see the sadness in their eyes. Of course, there are some who choose to continue working in another job because, "it keeps the mind healthy!"

Evidently, the lack of money is the main reason why so many continue to work even after retirement. Let me give you a picture of the average Malaysian lifestyle.

This is the story of Lawrence and Penny, a young couple with so much ahead of them, young, vibrant and full of promise. Their love for each other is indisputable. They have promised each other that they will look after each other for the rest of their lives.

Outside the offices of the Singer Sewing Machine and Courts Mammoth, two of the largest 'buy now pay later' or 'hire-purchase' schemes in the country, there is a prominent signboard advertising the schemes. Their jingles and TV commercials are also incredibly inviting.

Lawrence is a young executive who works in a bank as an assistant and takes home RM2000 monthly, and Penny, his wife, works in a sawmill as an administrator with a paycheck of RM1800. Like many new house owners, they made their way to the nearest outlet of the scheme with their income tax return forms or bank statements for their credit-check in order to qualify for the scheme.

Lawrence looked at the big screen TV while Penny went around the bedroom set. After an hour of inspection, they had made up their minds, Lawrence went in for the 43" TV set, whose tag indicated only RM83.15 per week while Penny decided on the American Oakwood king size bed, with a tag of RM22.50 per week.

"Seems like a good deal. Only RM22.50 per week, Lawrence..." Penny convinced herself, while Lawrence justified it by saying, "We need this big screen TV with this, I can at least have a decent TV to place in our empty hall so that visitors who come can see it!"

What makes Lawrence and Penny so vulnerable at the time of purchase?

"It's only RM105.65 per week."

They calculated their income, and found they could afford it. Yes, and nothing was going to stop them! After all, with their combined income, they get something like RM3800 per month. And what is RM422.60 per month for beautifying their home?

The original price of the 43" TV is RM9000, but in the live-purchase scheme, after three years of struggle, they will pay RM11700 (10% on interest). And at the end of the third year, it they want to sell it, they will be lucky if they can get RM3000. The sad part of the scenario was that Lawrence was actually buying a TV set that he really can afford now, but was imposing upon their future income to funding it. The hire-purchase company takes home a clean RM2900 from Lawrence's deal. Now, this is only a TV set. I have not mentioned that for the RM160000 house they had just moved into they would have a mortgage of RM1500 for the next 25 years. For Proton Waja, which they had bought a year ago, they took a loan for seven years that would come to something like RM680 per month.

The bottom line is that RM2602 is spent from the RM3800 (their total income), leaving something like less than a thousand Ringgit after deducting their monthly contribution payment to the employees provident fund. Like all young couples and homemakers, Lawrence and Penny spend their weekends at the malls. They say it is window-shopping, but on an average, they spend RM20 weekly just on petrol, parking and some refreshments at the mall.

I haven't mentioned the cost of their daily food consumption, and other utilities that they incur monthly. The truth is they can't make ends meet.

So, what's the solution? Juggling of funds, that's the next best thing to do. They turn to the plastic card that is stylishly displayed in their wallets. And begin spending more of the money, they hope to earn in the future. The credit card company wants you to pay only the minimum payment, and if you skip a month in repayment, they actually rejoice, for a simple reason that they can take more off you in financial charges, and for late payment. Has it occurred to you that the bank that offers you a credit card, makes a huge profit from late payment alone? Suppose that there are 400,000 card-holders, and 50% of them make late payments for which they are charged only RM5. Just think about the staggering figure. 200000 X RM5, that's a million a month! That's right, RM12 million a year. Incredible, isn't it? That's why they can afford to come up with the most inviting advertisements in the newspaper and TV commercials, influencing young people into believing like Lawrence that owning a credit card is a sign of success.

Lawrence feels a surge of success each time he whips out his credit card and Penny too, does her weekly grocery shopping with her credit cards. They kept their promise and made a minimum payment monthly. The compound interest kept adding up in their card statements, and soon, before they could make any alteration in their spending habits, the statement indicated a five-figure outstanding unpaid bill. For ten years, they lived comfortably, so to speak, then one day, Lawrence came home with the bad news that he had been retrenched.

To cut the story short, Lawrence and Penny had many arguments over money, and were divorced five years later. Lawrence was declared bankrupt by the credit card company because the amount was way too high for him to settle and he ended up as a shop assistant working in a motorcycle retail shop in Petaling Jaya, while Penny remarried, and spent a quiet life being careful with her expenditure from then on.

Do you think that what happened to Lawrence and Penny could have been avoided if only they had been a little thrifty in their expenditure?

Quite frankly, Lawrence and Penny didn't have to live their lives this way; they could have made their lives a whole lot easier by not having so many commitments. Both the TV and bedroom set were mistakes. They could have settled for something a lot cheaper. After all, beautifying a home is a life long exercise, and should be done only when funds allow it. Obviously, the credit card was their killer.

What Lawrence and Penny should have done was to keep aside RM380 per month (10% of their monthly income) as saving. If they had done that, they would have had some

RM68400 to get by during the retrenchment of Lawrence. And you know what? The divorce could have been avoided.

The story of Lawrence and Penny is very real for all of us. In my tours around the world, I have met so many people who come to my seminars. Their appearance tells me only one-thing: they are searching for ways to take action today that will enable them to have a breakthrough tomorrow. I have seen so many people whose marriages failed because of financial difficulties.

THERE IS AN OLD SAYING;
SAVE YOUR MONEY FOR A RAINY DAY

I have seen men and women who were driven to desperation by financial nightmares, driven to despondency, with some of them becoming suicidal. Financial development is very much like building a highway, it can't be done overnight, it is a day-to-day affair. It requires discipline and a lot of motivation.

Savings is another major concern of another group of hyper-individuals. These are the sales agents in life insurance and network marketing distributors, who in the past made so much money, but only a few managed to save some.

Like in a classical case, which I have shared many times over in seminars: there are people who spent some RM30000 on a down-payment for a S-class Benz, and took a loan with monthly repayment of RM4000 for the next six years while their five kids were squeezed into one small room, because they live in a two-room apartment. Incredible, isn't it? But it's true. This man is still around today and living in the same apartment, but he is no longer the proud owner of the S-Class.

We can begin by being a little thrifty in our day-to-day expenses, begin saving the 10% from our monthly paycheck now! Here's what you need to do right now.

If your credit card statement shows a five-figure unpaid bill, and you don't have the capacity to pay up in full, then I suggest that you cut down the use of the card, or better still don't use it until you have settled the entire amount shown in the statement. Or you can return the card to the owner (bank) and let them know that you wish to terminate it but will continue to settle the amount. If you have the money to pay up in full, do it right away! And apply for a charge card instead. Why am I suggesting these steps to you? Because you have unique spending habits, that's why!

Is your car loan overdue? If yes, then there is a problem. By rights, you should be at least two or three months ahead of the loan, the same goes for your house. That way, you will never be caught in any financial situation for too long.

Lastly, be thrifty in everything. Unnecessary lavish spending can offer you only temporary satisfaction. Saving little by little will take you far! Whoever you are, whether you are earning a four-figure or even a seven-figure income, it is time to ask for some advice on financial planning.

Success Principle #9

Be Available

*"Are you available
when someone is in need?
Can you count on yourself?"*

Be Available

In 1982, after attending a workshop in San Diego, and the next workshop being a few days later, I took a trip to Las Vegas and stayed at the Plaza. The memory has never left me. The millions of lighted bulbs that brightened the entire hotel left a lasting impression on me. The hotel put me on the upper floor, and I had a clear view of the entire area. I thought to myself at that point of time that I was really very fortunate to be able to come to Las Vegas and that some day when I had a family of my own, I would like them to see this great place as well. At the end of 2002, together with my family, we booked five tickets to the US. It was my three children's first trip to the USA.

A few nights before our departure, I went into my study and took out my journal, to refer back to the places I had visited some 20 years ago. Inevitably, Las Vegas and the photo of myself taken at the Plaza were there. I told my family that visiting Las Vegas would be part of our itinerary this time. 18th December 2002, my family and I arrived in Las Vegas. The booking agent had booked us into one of the hotels at the 'strip', it was obviously a much bigger and better hotel than the Plaza. Almost all the hotels in Las Vegas are equipped with entertainment for children, from riding the mega roller coaster, to the most powerful virtual play-game. Our kids went wild with it all, while Judy and I watched, and captured every moment of joy in our digital camera.

One morning, I hailed a taxi and told the driver that we wished to visit the Plaza. When we arrived at the Plaza, I found that almost everything had changed. The hotel stood elegantly as before, except it was now an old building which needed a new coat of paint.

"Kids, I want you to know that your dad actually stayed at this hotel some 20 years ago," I began.

"I was here all alone at that time, and I told myself that some day when I had a family of my own, I would want them to visit this hotel," I reiterated.

"Are there any rides in this hotel?" my youngest daughter, Delena asked.

"No, there are no rides in this hotel, it is just a simple old casino hotel," I explained.

"Then, why are we here dad?" she asked again.

"Darling, I just want all of you to know that I am available for you now. And if anything needs to be done, I shall get it done, because I am available. But some day, if I am not here anymore, then things will be a little different," I tried to explain in the simplest manner.

Are you available to do the things that need to be done? Fools live on promises while achievers ensure availability at all times. Can your children count on you to live a life filled with promises? We have a simple rule at home. When the kids have any problem with their schoolwork – they go to their mother! Dad can't help out. However, if they run into any other problem or challenge, dad is available at all times!

Do your children look at you and see a ray of hope or do they see a man preoccupied with many important things, for whom they are least important? Because you are not available for them when they need you. Can they really count on you?

I am not saying I am the best dad in the world. As a matter of fact, most of the dads and moms I know sincerely want to be the best and also provide the best for their children. So, they get out there to buy them the most expensive toys, food is plentiful at all times and they ensure that there are no hiccups in school. Buying your children toys and giving them the best education does not make you the best dad or mom. It is your availability that does.

BE AVAILABLE

FOR THOSE

WHO NEED YOU

BE ON STAND-BY

FOR THOSE

WHO DO NOT NEED YOU

They need hugs from you, they need to hear how much you love them and treasure them. They need to be constantly aware of how much you cherish them, and that you are there for them all the time.

Can someone count on you at work? Are you available as an employee? Can your superior in your workplace entrust you with a task without having to check on you? There are so many 'passenger' employees out there, always waiting for a 'free-lunch', their entire working career is a free ride. They try to outsmart their employer. Clock-watching, disappearing from work and finding excuses not to show up – such are their trademarks. Their greatest joy in their job is payday, for they have no challenge whatsoever in performing a task given at the workplace.

No, these employees are not available. And their trademarks are normally short-lived. In the event of a financial crisis, these 'passenger' employees will be the first to go. And when they are axed, they blame the entire world for the cruel and unjust execution.

Do yourself a favour; if you are one of these 'passenger' employees, it is time to begin paying for the ride. Be available, and make yourself an important and useful person. Such worth is rare these days.

As children, are you available to your parents? Many of our Asian cultures are being transformed. We are beginning to forget our cultures because of the great influence of the western media, and the free flow of western movies that flood our minds, that brainwash our thoughts, and change some of our perceptions about life. We become defiant and rebellious, both against the law and the family.

As children, what does it take to be available? Discipline! You don't really need to be reminded to do your schoolwork. You don't really need to be reminded to go to school. Neither do you need to be reminded of your aim in life.

Being available is to allow your children to do the things we did when we were young. Today, we enjoy such luxuries; it is no wonder the children are spoiled. Today, almost every home in the country employs a live-in maid, who is paid to do virtually everything, from laying the table to cleaning the bathrooms. Children need to be available when the dinner is over, helping to clear the table, and clean the dishes. However, most mothers don't think of it that way, they prefer the children to concentrate on their studies while the chores are taken care of by the maid. I am not saying you need to have your children do these chores every day. Just once in a while will do. That's being available! Mothers, you will be glad that they are.

Success Principle #10

Start Loving and Stop Fighting

" If there is love,
impossible will
become possible. "

Start Loving and Stop Fighting

I chose to keep this principle as the last of the 10 principles of success. It is also the most powerful principle ever known to humankind. I believe all of us have this principle in us, but we don't take full advantage of it, which explains why there are so many people who are still struggling and striving for 'eternal happiness.'

One of the deadliest diseases in the world today is not HIV, neither cancer nor heart disease. To me, the deadliest disease in the modern world is living a dead life. A life that is filled with hatred, greed, and hostility, always fighting over something. Literally, millions of people are suffering from this disease.

Have you come across people who complain just about everything? From the moment they get up in the morning till they retire at night, complaining is their major pastime. They fight with anyone who comes their way. They complain about their kids, they fight with their colleagues, their employers and subordinates, and blame the government for not doing enough. Just about everything under the sky. These people continue to harbour ill feelings, for themselves as well for others. Generally, they are not happy people, for they do not know what happiness really is.

They are envious of what others have, they are victims and prisoners of frustration and disappointment. They always run down others who are doing much better than them, and they will never be satisfied with what they have. They suffer from a poor self-image, and enjoy giving everyone else a hard time.

The Bible says: "He that loveth not, knoweth not God, for God is Love." People who suffer from this deadly disease have only one cure, and that is the perpetual melody of humanity known as love.

After those years of searching, I have finally found the ultimate answer to true happiness. It is not money, nor power or the titles bestowed by kings and clergymen but rather the holiest emotion of our souls, the golden link which binds us to our duty and to the truth – love.

Love will eliminate, reject and destroy greed, hatred, jealousy and ego, and will instantly build harmony, bring smiles to our faces, and chip away the wall of pretence that we erect as a defence mechanism.

Start loving today and stop fighting with yourself. If you look around, you will see these lonely people who lack this 'link' to their happiness, joy and even success. Every human being who is lonely and wretched, and aspires for happiness and contentment, feels the need for love. Without love, our life is incomplete and hopeless without an aim, and we become miserable.

Love is a great instrument of nature, it bonds and cements our society, it is the spirit and spring of this great universe. At the time of writing, the USA, under the leadership of President George W Bush, was pushing relentlessly ahead with the war against Iraq. Who can stop the war? Love can. If both parties are willing, if both parties are filled with a little bit of love. If you look at these two dignitaries, President Bush and President Saddam Hussien, what is missing here? Love. Yes, only love can stop the war now. But then again, it is easier said than done. Take, for example, two vicious dogs engaged in combat, each defiant of the other. There is no time to establish love. When the latch is released, they fight each other until one falls flat on the ground, and the other walks away with more pride than ever. However, given the time, we can train these two dogs to be brothers rather than enemies. For love, time is of the essence.

LIFE IS THE FLOWER

OF WHICH LOVE

IS THE HONEY

During my vacation with my family in Japan, I came across a beautiful scroll written by Sekio, a man who was dying from cancer. From his death bed he wrote: "When time brings us to the resting place of life – as we expect, and in some measure, attain them, when we stop to consider the way and study its import, we will look back over the waste ground which we leave behind. Is it a bright spot? Is it where the star of love has shed its beams? Is there a plant or flower, or any beautiful thing visible? Or is it where the smiles and tears of affection have been spent – where some fond eye met our own, some endearing heart was clasped to ours? Take these away and what joy has memory in retrospection, or what delight has hope in future prospects? The bosom which does not feel love is cold; the mind which does not conceive is dull; the philosophy which does not accept is false; and only that religion is pure and reciprocal which has undying love as its basis. The love that makes the memory happy and the home beautiful from the sunlight of our earlier years, it beams gratefully along the pathway of our mature years, and the radiance lingers until the shadows of death darken it."

Yes, love conquers all. Stop fighting and start to live a life of love. Every day send out the love within us, and when this purified energy comes back, it comes back manifold. One of my students once asked: "How do we develop love?"

Start looking for the goodness in everyone who comes your way, and erase the ego within you, and slowly and gradually you will become a loving person, full of fun.

Every Adversity Has a Silver Lining

Perhaps, it was a blessing in disguise that I failed my L.C.E. examination in 1969. Perhaps, it was a blessing that I started working as an unskilled labourer in the beginning. These setbacks actually forced me to get up and move. It was a circumstance beyond my control then. Nobody wants to fail in an exam, neither does anyone want to labour under a merciless, hot sun daily.

Stay Focussed and Fight One More Round

For many, failing in their basic education academic exam is an adversity that is often used as an excuse for their failures. For the past 25 years as a speaker, I have had the privilege to travel and study people in different situations, some were most unfortunate, others...blessed in many ways.

I believe most of us go through some kind of trial before we achieve success. Success is achieved by constant belief, commitment and desire. Somewhere along the way, many are forced to take another route because of certain challenges, but, the final objective must be met, no matter what it takes, and no matter how long it takes. It must be accomplished! Quitting is the easiest way out. Never in the history of mankind was a statue erected in memory of a quitter. If you are already out there with a plan for success and wish to quit now, then welcome to the world of quitters, whose names will be forgotten in a very short time. Success is not a game of chance, it must be directed, focussed with a well-laid out plan of action.

Secret of Success

Much depend largely on how much interest you have in what you do. In business, at home and in the community, the successful combination is Do What You Do Better With Interest and Do More Of What You Do Best! That has been my philosophy and is the secret of my success in a nutshell. As I reveal to you this blueprint, my intention is pretty obvious. I am certain that you want to achieve a higher percentage of success in what you are doing at the moment, don't you? If the successful accomplishment of a task or job is what you are after, then I shall explain further these two maxims.

Do What You Do Better With Interest

These days I spend some time on the 'green' playing golf with friends and associates. Many of them have asked me: "David, what's the secret of your success?" And my reply has always been the same.

"Brother, you got a job?"

"Yes..." they reply.

"Do you enjoy working there?" I probe further.

"Yes!"

"Keep working with a heart," I advised.

It does not matter if you are an employee or self-employed. The point here is that whatever we do, we must do it with a heart, which is interest! Whether you are a typist, clerk, accounts executive or a manager of a division, the first thing you need to understand is that there is always a time and place for everything. Don't try to fly when you have just learned to walk. When you work for others, I know it is with the hope that some day, you will be self-employed. If you come in this category, then I suggest that you narrow down your thoughts and focus on a special skill (here, I am referring to what you are offering, the service in the industry, of which there is no stock piling up in a warehouse), master it, be really good at it. Stay at it for some time and save a substantial amount of money that will last you at least a year with no income. When you have this self-sustaining 'stamina' then, you will be ready to take on the self-employed position.

Here's a suggestion. Don't get involved in any network marketing or life insurance company if you are not ready. By this I mean that if you are still working hard at your job, and thinking you want to try out something which could earn you extra income – my advice is, don't do it! Many people have tried it, and failed. Why? Network marketing and life insurance, both these trades need great commitment. They need focus, determination and lots of interest. Unless, you are disciplined and interested in meeting new prospects daily, and have a hunger for financial success, I suggest you continue working in your office and focus on your progress and promotion there. However, if you think you want to try out network marketing or life insurance, then go out there, and divide your time appropriately. Stay on the job and after office hours, sell, sponsor/recruit and be able to service as time goes by. It has to be done with love (interest). Initially, like all things, the trade will be difficult. Gradually, you will learn the trade, and you will succeed. But stay focussed, and be disciplined.

Do More Of What You Do Best

The second maxim render more service! Whatever you are doing at this moment, be really good at it, and render more of your services to the people, the company and towards your experience. Money is important, but there are times in life when money can't be included in the subject. Rendering more of our service costs money and involves effort. But we need to do it.

There are thousands of ATMs (Automated Teller Machine) in this country. These machines allow you to withdraw money at your convenience. The banks do not make a cent for providing these, and you know something? Each ATM costs approximately RM350,000–RM500,000. They are there to serve you. Service – Do More Of What You Do Best!

Epilogue

As The Curtain Rises

Action speaks louder than words. Great knowledge without action amounts to nothing. It has to be followed with action. Nothing begins by itself, this is the law of nature. I remember when I was young and selling ice-cream, my mother once told me "Son, if you are just going to stare at those ice-cream cones, nothing will be sold. You need to walk out there to sell them." I couldn't agree more, everything needs action. All those mechanical gadgets or electronic appliances we use daily have to be triggered off by action. Your home is cooled automatically, but you must select (action) the temperature you want. The same principle applies to the 'mind' action. When you are in the right frame of mind, it can help you produce the desired results.

Every big job – whether it is in business, high-level selling, science, network marketing, conventional selling or in government – everything requires a man of action. We see this almost everyday in our local newspapers. In the classified section, companies are looking for self-motivated employees. And just what do they mean by a 'self-motivated' employee? Yes, that's right! A man or woman of action. Ideas are an excellent commodity, but not good enough if action does not follow. If you think about it for a moment, everything we have in this world, from the skyscraper to the satellite, the laundry powder to the toothpick, are the results of an idea acted upon. How often we have heard a story of someone telling another about a certain product or service: "I thought about that idea or service a long time ago… I should have done something about it then."

If you really want to succeed in life, there is no room for: "Yes, I would like to start, but…"

Have you got a good idea? Do something about it now. Last Sunday, my Pastor, Rev. Philip Tan said: "Those poor people, they are poor not because they don't have money, but because they don't have an idea that can be put into action."

Remember the 10 success principles that I have recorded in this book. I know if I had not acted on the idea to be a better speaker and writer, I would still be in a construction firm somewhere in the city today.

There is No Time To Waste

I was just going through a VCD of mine made in Taiwan several years ago. I noticed one of the most visible things that had changed in my appearance was the colour of my hair. In the past five years, my hair has greyed so much, and I think to myself, "Wow, David, you have just turned 50 this year…" Time flies. Seems as if it wasn't long ago that I used to look up at the black sky at night staring at the three stars that lay so still in a row. I used to talk to these three stars, and I would go out and seek for an answer when things went terribly wrong in my life, when I was a kid. These three stars had been a constant companion in my life. I told my kids about these three stars when we were in our garden one night. **The three-star saga, that was a long time ago…** Today as we grow older, our values change, our perception is no longer as sentimental as we would like to, and our feelings toward others have changed to be more serene, caring and perhaps…more willing. That is of course when we have achieved the things we want and attain the ability to offer. To really accomplish something, we need to start doing it now. Maybe, it's a house or a car or a boat that you want to own earnestly. Whatever it is, start getting into action. **You know what!** Begin by saving a little money from your paycheck every month. Do it now! Some day, when you get older, you will understand what I am talking about.

Be a doer, and an achiever. Be someone who makes things happen and not someone who merely watches. Don't wait for the right time, it never comes. Expect unforeseen obstacles and challenges ahead and solve them as they arise. Take each day as if it were your last, and offer the best you can in whatever you do.

My books are read by millions of people today. Someone once told me that I will not be able to succeed as an author. I didn't believe that individual. I believed in God, who blessed me generously. When you ardently believe in something, it will become a reality, if you put in the effort.

Other books by the same author

Network Marketing

Effective Sponsoring Skills

Making a Career

52 Ways to Make More Money
in Network Marketing

Self-Improvement Series for Sales People

Blue Print for Greater Success (*Forthcoming*)

The Making of a Super Salesperson

Start Selling Stop Order Taking

Secrets of a Top Sales Performer